LCVP LINK MODULES

Making It Happen

Caroline McHale

This book is dedicated to my lovely parents, Margaret and Peter McHale.

Editor
Kristin Jensen

Cover Design
Suzanne Gannon

Design and Layout
Suzanne Gannon

ISBN 978-1-78090-422-1

Folens Publishers
Hibernian Industrial Estate
Greenhills Road
Tallaght
Dublin 24

The author and publisher wish to thank the following for permission to reproduce copyright material: Aviva; Bank of Ireland; iStockphoto; Jack & Jill Children's Foundation; Photocall Ireland; SIPTU; TidyTowns Unit, Department of the Environment, Community and Local Government.

CONTENTS

■ Introduction   v

■ Learning Template for LCVP   vii

■ Mind Map: Outline of the LCVP Link Modules   viii

Section 01 — PEP – An Integrated Learning Approach

■ Introduction to PEP: Pre-experience, Experience and Post-experience   **1**

■ Pre-experience   **3**

   Planning: Enterprise/action plan   3

   Planning for LCVP activities: Enterprise/action plan   4

■ Enterprise/action plan guidelines   **4**

■ Enterprise/action plan template   **6**

   Checklist for success criteria for an enterprise/action plan   7

■ Sample portfolio entry   **8**

■ Experience   **9**

   Visit in   9

   Visit out   10

■ Cross-curricular – link the learning   **11**

   Linkages between your vocational subject groupings (VSGs)   11

   Linkages between your vocational subject groupings and other Leaving Certificate subjects   11

   Linkages between subjects and the wider community (e.g. work placements, visits out, career investigations)   11

■ What are your LCVP skills and qualities?   **12**

   Qualities   12

   Skills in the Link Modules classroom   12

   Sample of skills and their uses in LCVP   12

■ Post-experience – evaluation   **14**

   Why evaluate?   15

   How to evaluate LCVP activities   15

■ Summary report   **16**

■ Template: Summary report based on a Link Modules activity   **17**

■ Summary report template   **18**

   Checklist for success criteria for the summary report   19

■ Twenty sample questions   **20**

CONTENTS

Section 02 — Link Module 1 – Preparation for the World of Work

- Unit 1 – Introduction to Working Life 21
- Unit 2 – Job-seeking Skills 48
- Unit 3 – Career Investigation 71
- Unit 4 – Work Placement 93

Section 03 — Link Module 2 – Enterprise Education

- Unit 1 – Enterprise Skills 115
- Unit 2 – Local Business Enterprises 135
- Unit 3 – Local Voluntary Organisations and Community Enterprises 153
- Unit 4 – An Enterprise Activity 165

Section 04 — Assessment

- Overview of assessment 186
- LCVP Assessment 187
- Certification 188
  - Points 188
- Portfolio of coursework 189
  - Portfolio restrictions 189
  - Portfolio content 190
  - Ten tips for perfecting your portfolio items 190
- Portfolio: Comparison of reports 192
- The recorded interview/presentation 193
  - Recorded interview/presentation restrictions 193
  - Recorded interview 193
- Recorded interview/presentation template 195
- Score sheet for a recorded interview/presentation 196
- Recorded interview/presentation guidelines 197
  - Checklist for success criteria for the recorded interview/presentation 198
- The written examination 199
  - Section A: Audio-visual presentation (30 marks) 199
  - Section B: Case study (30 marks) 199
  - Section C: General questions (4 x 25 marks) 202
- Revising exam questions: Some important themes 202
  - Important tips 204
  - How to answer questions 205
- Possible marking scheme for core portfolio items 206
- Possible marking scheme for optional portfolio items 207
- LCVP assessment words 208

Introduction

The Leaving Certificate Vocational Programme (LCVP) is a senior cycle programme designed to give a strong vocational dimension to the Leaving Certificate. The focus of the LCVP is to prepare you for adult life by ensuring you are educated in the broadest sense possible. It will help you cope in the work environment or with further education or perhaps help you to establish an enterprise. It is an activity-based programme that helps you develop skills and gear you towards self-directed learning. It is an additional subject for the Leaving Certificate and students can achieve up to 70 points.

This book is an updated version of *Making It Happen*. The book is divided into four distinct sections and can be used in whatever order you prefer. You don't have to adhere to the book rigidly – you may opt to engage in different activities and select the relevant information in order to achieve the syllabus, which is written in specific learning outcomes (SLOs).

The programme is divided into two link modules: Preparation for the World of Work and Enterprise Education. These are best fostered through a range of activities. This book has an interesting approach to the activities, called the PEP approach. Section 1 clearly explains PEP, where every activity is broken down into three distinct phases: pre-experience, experience and post-experience, or before, during and after. An important feature is documenting your skills (see pages 12–14) while participating in the programme.

The two link modules, Preparation for the World of Work and Enterprise Education, are short courses. However they are treated as one for assessment purposes and the written paper is at common level. These are covered in Section 2 and Section 3.

Day to Day in the LCVP Classroom

- Use the learning template for your LCVP copy or folder (page vii). Draft the layout on a page in your LCVP copy or folder. Fill in the date (including year), topic, key words, key SLOs and document your skills. At the end of the class, write a good question, perhaps using the examination outcome verbs on page 208. Keep the main part of the template for main points. Try and keep to one page, as it's easier for revision.
- Draft a **Mind Map** on key topics to help you revise and prepare for the case study. Draw one or use an electronic version and fill in the information.
- Cover all the **SLOs**. They are ideal for revision, for starting a class to see what you already know, for designing questionnaires, for careers, for the 'My Own Place' report and for investigating entrepreneurs. They can also be part of the briefing for speakers to the classroom and preparing for outside visits. You may already be familiar with a number of the SLOs, but add to your knowledge and constantly revisit and update your notes.
- The **PEP approach** (pre-experience, experience, post-experience) should be applied for every activity. It encourages you to plan every activity (use the enterprise/action plan template on page 6), experience the activity (be sure to engage in every activity, as you always need to have an individual perspective) and finally, evaluate every activity (use the DAR approach – describe, assess and reflect – on page 15).
- The **learning boards** at the end of each unit are a great way to revise. The learning boards look at key questions, devise questions, encourage presentations, link the SLOs, revise the key words, document skills acquired, link the LCVP to other Leaving Certificate subjects and provide 20 sample questions to test your learning.

Learning in the LCVP

- View YouTube clips on key themes.
- Use search engines for key themes, as a lot of the information required is local to your own area. Be sure information is up to date, as the world of work and enterprise continually changes.
- Work in groups and individually. Always document group and individual learning.
- Practise presentations, which will help you prepare for your recorded interview/presentation.
- When completing the LCVP templates, activities, tasks, success criteria checklists and 20 sample questions, apply the three Ts:
  - **T**hink about your answer
  - **T**urn to your partner
  - **T**alk about your learning, explain and give an example

Ask for explanations if you are unclear.

The outline of the LCVP mind map on page viii gives a clear over view of the programme. Section 4 deals with assessment, where the portfolio is worth 60% and the written paper 40%.

When drafting portfolio items, follow these tips:

- Choose an appropriate LCVP activity that demonstrates skills. Document at least three skills. The activity must relate to an SLO.
- Copy the templates into your LCVP copies or folders. Use key words initially, then revisit, revise and articulate your learning.
- Follow the important guidelines. They will scaffold your learning. No excuses and you can't deviate.
- Embrace the ten tips for perfecting your portfolio on pages 190–91. Type up your portfolio items.
- Work in pairs. Use peer assessment and follow the success criteria checklists.
- Revisit your portfolio and make sure it is consistent and free of errors. Follow the tips on page 191.
- Remember, it must be an LCVP activity. Use the PEP approach. Articulate learning and a few key skills. Always link to the world of work, enterprise education and further education. Be specific and always give examples. If you are writing a summary report on the Jack & Jill Foundation, for example, it should be on a visit to the organisation or a visitor to the classroom from that organisation.

Practice makes perfect. While discussion is a good way to understand, improve learning and improve communication, you also need to document and write your answers. The written examination is worth a substantial amount of the marks (40%). The 20 sample questions at the end of the units will help you prepare for the examination.

Work in pairs and discuss answers, then write your answers down and see if your partner has any additional information. Practise frequently. Take out a blank sheet of paper and see if you can articulate the main points, explain them and give appropriate examples. Use your portfolio as a revision tool for the written exam. Always practise with past Leaving Certificate papers and view marking schemes to help you prepare for the final assessment.

Finally, I hope you will find this book useful as you participate in the programme. I wish you every success and most importantly, I hope you enjoy the LCVP experience.

Caroline McHale, 2014

Learning Template for LCVP

Draw this template into your LCVP folder/copy. This is an ideal way of structuring learning for most of your classes.

Date	Unit/Topic

Keywords

SLOs

-
-
-
-
-
-
-

Skills

-
-
-
-
-
-

Websites	

Questions

Mind Map: Outline of the LCVP Link Modules

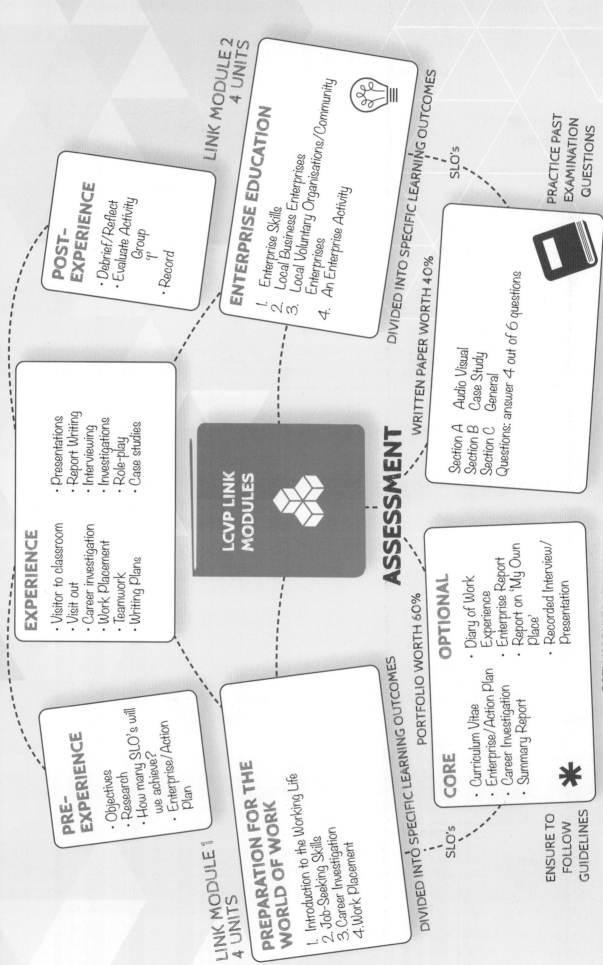

LINK MODULE 2
4 UNITS

POST-EXPERIENCE
· Debrief/Reflect
· Evaluate Activity
  Group
  '?'
· Record

ENTERPRISE EDUCATION
1. Enterprise Skills
2. Local Business Enterprises
3. Local Voluntary Organisations/Community Enterprises
4. An Enterprise Activity

DIVIDED INTO SPECIFIC LEARNING OUTCOMES

SLO's

PRACTICE PAST EXAMINATION QUESTIONS

EXPERIENCE
· Visitor to classroom
· Visit out
· Career investigation
· Work Placement
· Teamwork
· Writing Plans
· Presentations
· Report Writing
· Interviewing
· Investigations
· Role-play
· Case studies

LCVP LINK MODULES

ASSESSMENT

WRITTEN PAPER WORTH 40%

Section A   Audio Visual
Section B   Case Study
Section C   General
Questions: answer 4 out of 6 questions

PORTFOLIO WORTH 60%

CORE
· Curriculum Vitae
· Enterprise/Action Plan
· Career Investigation
· Summary Report

OPTIONAL
· Diary of Work Experience
· Enterprise Report
· Report on 'My Own Place'
· Recorded Interview/Presentation

PRE-EXPERIENCE
· Objectives
· Research
· How many SLO's will we achieve?
· Enterprise/Action Plan

PREPARATION FOR THE WORLD OF WORK
1. Introduction to the Working Life
2. Job-Seeking Skills
3. Career Investigation
4. Work Placement

LINK MODULE 1
4 UNITS

DIVIDED INTO SPECIFIC LEARNING OUTCOMES

SLO's

ENSURE TO FOLLOW GUIDELINES

BOTH MODULES ARE TREATED AS ONE FOR ASSESSMENT PURPOSES.
LINK THE LEARNING TO THE RELEVANT LEAVING CERTIFICATE SUBJECTS.

Introduction to PEP:
Pre-experience, Experience and Post-experience

The aim of this section is to help you develop an integrated approach to your study of the Link Modules. Through your two-year LCVP experience, you will participate in many different activities, such as visiting entrepreneurs, training schemes and voluntary organisations, inviting visitors to the classroom and a work placement. This book will help you to approach these activities in such a way that you will learn and gain as much as possible from each of them. This book outlines processes and procedures that can be applied to every activity you undertake, ensuring that you can use those activities to prepare your portfolio items and that you are adequately prepared for the written paper.

Each experience and activity in this book can be broken up into three PEP parts:

pre-experience, **e**xperience and **p**ost-experience, or before, during and after.

In order to make each experience as rich and as useful as possible, you should always start by preparing for the activity, move on to participating in the activity and finish by evaluating it.

As you will see from the diagram on the next page, there is as much, if not more, work required of you before and after the experience as during it.

Remember, you must take responsibility for your own learning:

- Plan your experience, perhaps using the enterprise/action plan template on page 6.
- Participate in your experience.
- Reflect on and evaluate your experience.
- Record your learning and document the skills gained.

Keep an **LCVP folder or copybook** and record your learning using the templates and ideas demonstrated in this book. After two years of using this book and the templates and activities in it, you will be adequately prepared for assessment. Use the templates to document key words, revisit and elaborate upon them and record them in your **LCVP folder**. Remember, key words are not acceptable in the examination – you must use sentences. As you type up your portfolio entries, make sure they are **free of errors**.

P.E.P.

PRE-EXPERIENCE EXPERIENCE POST-EXPERIENCE

BEFORE DURING AFTER

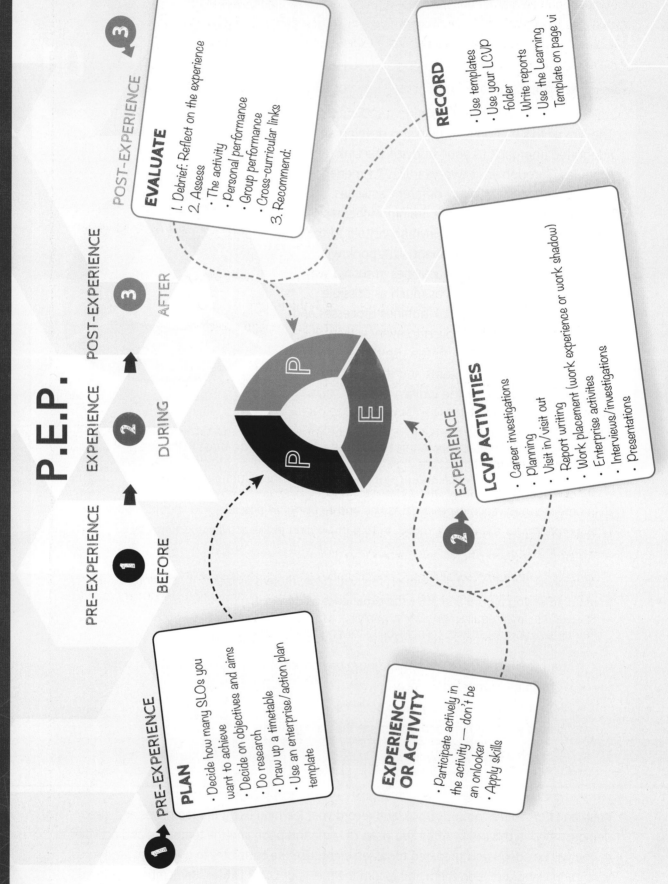

PRE-EXPERIENCE

PLAN
- Decide how many SLOs you want to achieve
- Decide on objectives and aims
- Do research
- Draw up a timetable
- Use an enterprise/action plan template

EXPERIENCE OR ACTIVITY
- Participate actively in the activity — don't be an onlooker
- Apply skills

EXPERIENCE

LCVP ACTIVITIES
- Career investigations
- Planning
- Visit in/visit out
- Report writing
- Work placement (work experience or work shadow)
- Enterprise activites
- Interviews/investigations
- Presentations

POST-EXPERIENCE

EVALUATE
1. Debrief: Reflect on the experience
2. Assess
   - The activity
   - Personal performance
   - Group performance
   - Cross-curricular links
3. Recommend:

RECORD
- Use templates
- Use your LCVP folder
- Write reports
- Use the Learning Template on page vi

Pre-experience

Participating in an activity that you are prepared for is a far more rewarding experience than participating in one that you are not prepared for. Preparing not only guarantees that you will enjoy the experience more, but that you will also gain more from it.

Planning: Enterprise/Action Plan

'A plan without action is a dream. Action without a plan is a nightmare.'
– Chinese proverb

The ability to **plan** effectively is a useful skill for you at school, at home and in the community. It is a skill that will also help you prepare for future studies and is a necessary skill for employment and starting your own business.

Planning is an important element of the LCVP and is part of the **learning cycle**.

- A plan refers to an activity that may take place in the future.
- It is a series of steps to be taken in order to achieve aims and objectives.
- It is a written document.

As an LCVP student, you must be aware of and understand two kinds of plans:

1. **Business plan** – written examination only (see pages 139–41).
2. **Enterprise/action plan** – core portfolio item **and/or** written examination (see pages 4–7).

There are many **reasons** to prepare a plan:

- It helps you to make informed decisions based on careful research and analysis.
- It establishes targets and describes how to achieve those targets.
- It helps to focus for the future and identify resources needed.
- It helps to raise questions and anticipate solutions.
- It analyses strengths, weaknesses, opportunities and threats/challenges (SWOT).
- It provides a benchmark (a standard to compare against) for evaluating performances.
- It is an essential requirement when applying for bank loans and grants.
- It can indicate whether or not you should go ahead with your idea.

Remember, disagreements can arise when planning activities. To overcome differences:

1. Your LCVP teacher could act as a mediator who listens to both sides and issues recommendations.
2. Define everyone's role in the planning stage. Ensure it is communicated clearly and this should reduce disagreements.
3. Have a meeting and perhaps set up smaller teams rather than individuals to take responsibility.

Planning for LCVP Activities: Enterprise/Action Plan

Before starting any LCVP activity, it is important to do some pre-experience work. This can be achieved by an enterprise/action plan. This plan is for an enterprise activity or an action that you intend to do in the LCVP. The action must be related to one or more of the **s**pecific **l**earning **o**utcomes (SLOs). Examples may include:

- A plan for a 'My Own Place' investigation
- A plan for a visitor to the LCVP classroom
- An LCVP plan for a visit out to a local business or voluntary organisation

> You may plan lots of activities in the LCUP, but you must do the research.

Enterprise/Action Plan Guidelines

Title	This should state that the document is an LCVP plan and indicate its purpose. Use a preface if required to link with the specific learning outcomes (SLOs).
Objectives **Group** **Personal** (personal is a must)	Include three objectives. They should refer to what you (or the group) expect to achieve or what you (or the group) hope to learn. If it is a group activity, you should include a personal objective. **Use the future tense.** It is a good idea to include a skills objective, e.g. 'I hope to improve my communication skills, develop my research skills and work on my IT skills.'

Research methods
 	
Group
 	
Personal
(personal a must)
	Include three different research methods. Make sure to include at least one personal research method. For example:
	
	   ■ Writing or telephoning for information
	   ■ Library or internet search
	   ■ Using a questionnaire
	
	Use the future tense.

Gap in Time: Stop and Conduct Research

Analysis of research **Group personal**	Summarise the outcome of each research method in a logical sequence. Record the relevant information obtained and how it will influence the plan. Be sure to elaborate and allow for additional research. **Use the past tense.**
Actions	Outline steps to implement the plan. Have at least five actions: one action prior to the event and detailed actions on the day of the activity. **Use the future tense.**
Schedule of time (actions and schedule of time can be combined)	Indicate how much time will be allocated to each part of the activity and the dates of any deadlines that must be met in order to carry out the plan. Include more detail closer to the time. **Use the future tense.**
Resources and costs	This may include materials and personnel. Material resources should be itemised and estimated costs recorded (e.g. 'We will incur the following…'). Include details, e.g. a table of costings. **Use the future tense.**
Evaluation methods **Group** **Personal** (link each one to each objective)	These are the methods or indicators you (or the group) plan to use to ascertain whether or not the objectives have been achieved. They must refer back to the stated objectives (1, 2 and 3). Make sure each objective is evaluated in a logical sequence and allow for detailed analysis. In the case of a group activity, you should include a method of evaluating the extent to which your personal objective has been achieved. **Use the future tense.**

Use this template to plan all LCVP activities. This will ensure that you have a choice of plans when completing your portfolio. Revise the ten tips for perfecting your portfolio items on pages 190–91.

Present revenue and costings in a tabulated format and make sure you understand surplus/profit or deficit/loss.

Resources and Costs:

Revenue	€	€
Sales	1,000.00	
Sponsorship	500.00	1,500.00
Costs		
Email & internet	60.00	
Stationery	5.40	
Advertising	100.00	165.40
Surplus/ profit		1,334.60

Tip: 300–600 words

Enterprise/Action Plan Template

Title	
Objectives	
Research methods	
Analysis of research	
Actions	
Schedule of time	
Resources and costs	
Evaluation methods	

Tip: This is the only part of the Plan which is written in the past.

All Portfolio items must be consistent, use a space after a full stop. All headings size 14 bold, Times New Roman size 12 for the remainder, use tabs, ensure grammar is correct, indent, no spelling mistakes and consistency with bullet points, numbering, etc.

Checklist for success criteria for an enterprise/action plan

When you have finished your enterprise/action plan, read the list below to make sure you fulfil the LCVP requirements. Be sure to elaborate and articulate each portfolio item. Go to Section 4: Assessment to check general rules for the portfolio and apply the ten tips for perfecting your portfolio items on pages 190–91.

- ✓ Is your plan word-processed?
- ✓ Did you check that the word count is between 300 and 600 words?
- ✓ Is your plan written in the future tense (with the exception of the 'Analysis of Research section, which must be written in the past tense)?
- ✓ Have you been consistent in your use of punctuation, capitals, font, underlining, etc.?
- ✓ Have you checked for spelling and grammar errors?
- ✓ Did you state your name as the author?
- ✓ Have you checked the layout and presentation, as suggested in the guidelines?
- ✓ Have you stated the title, an LCVP plan and the purpose of the plan?
- ✓ Did you state at least three different objectives?
- ✓ Have you included at least one personal objective as well as two group objectives?
- ✓ Have you stated at least three different types of research methods?
- ✓ Did you analyse each research method you carried out? Did you clearly state the outcomes using the past tense? Did you allow for additional research?
- ✓ Have you stated the action steps you will now need to take to complete the activity?
- ✓ Did you state how long each of these action steps will take?
- ✓ Have you stated all the resources and costs involved?
- ✓ Have you written full sentences?
- ✓ Did you state what evaluation methods you will put in place to achieve your plan?
- ✓ Did you state how you will know if you achieve your objectives?
- ✓ Have you linked all the evaluation methods you will use to all your objectives?
- ✓ Proofread your enterprise/action plan to make sure it is free of errors and as perfect as possible.

Work in pairs and use this checklist to evaluate your portfolio. Ask for explanations.

Sample Portfolio Entry

ENTERPRISE/ACTION PLAN

PLAN FOR AN LCVP FUNDRAISING EVENT

A plan to organise a school disco to raise money for Trócaire as part of our enterprise activity for LCVP.

Objectives

- We want to plan an LCVP fundraising activity to raise money for Trócaire.
- We hope that the LCVP class will work well as a team.
- I hope to fulfil part of the LCVP course by doing a personal plan. I hope to improve my planning skills, work on my communication skills and develop my organisational skills.

Research Methods

- I will arrange a meeting with our principal to get permission to hold the disco and to arrange a suitable date, time, DJ and any other requirements for a disco.
- We will do a survey in school to identify how many students would be interested in attending a school disco.
- I will use the internet to research modern music tastes and the top 30 singles in Ireland presently.

Analysis of Research

- After my meeting with the principal, we have permission to hold the disco in the school hall on Friday, 16 October 2015, from 8pm until 11pm. I have arranged for a DJ, Steven Dunford, at a competitive price of €130.00.
- From our survey, out of approximately 450 students in the school, 370 said they would attend a school disco.
- I used the internet to download the top 30 singles and I hope to continue researching this subject as part of my Music course for my Leaving Certificate.

Actions

- I will ask teachers if they are available to supervise on the night.
- I will confirm DJ Steven Dunford at our agreed price.
- We will draft and distribute posters around the school.
- We will organise a clean-up in the hall.
- We must divide up the workload on the night and after the disco.
- We will clean up the hall after the disco.
- I will arrange a meeting with a representative from Trócaire to organise handing over the money we will have raised from this LCVP fundraising activity.

Schedule of Time

- 6 October 2015: I will ask teachers if they are available to
- 7 October 2015: I will book the DJ for that night and ag
- 9 October 2015: We will make posters to advertise the
- 16 October 2015: We will agree jobs to be carried out
  disco, e.g. cloakroom, shop.
- 17 October 2015: Day of disco.
  - –2.00pm Clean hall
  - –3.30pm Stick tickets beside each hanger in cloak
  - –7.20pm Reopen school and help DJ carry in equi
  - –7.45pm Take floats for front door and cloakroom
  - –8.00pm Open doors
  - –8.30pm Close doors
  - –11.00pm End disco
  - –11.15pm Clean up hall
  - –11.30pm Once hall is cleaned, have school
- 24 October 2015: I will arrange a meeting wi

Res

- Resources: Teachers, LCVP team and car
- Revenue: Expected revenue from entry
  cloakroom)
- Costs:

DJ	€130.00
Cloakroom tickets	€ 7.50
	€ 10.00
Posters	€ 1.20
Phone calls	€148.70
Total	

Proposed money for charity = €1,351.30

Evaluation Methods

- If we raise our target of €1,351.30, then we will have achieved our objective of raising money for Trócaire.
- If we complete this activity according to plan, we will have demonstrated excellent team skills. We will ask our LCVP teacher to evaluate our team and what team skills we demonstrated.
- If I can write an enterprise/action plan according to the assessment criteria, I will have achieved my personal objective.
- If this activity runs according to plan, I will have demonstrated my planning and organisation skills. I will ask both my music teacher and the Trócaire representative to comment on both these skills. These will help me with future studies, in the world of work and if I ever decide to establish my own music business.
- If we achieve all our objectives, we will have been successful in planning this activity.

Tip: Ensure you do the research and write it in the past tense.

Experience

Visit In

LCVP activities, e.g. a visit from an entrepreneur.

Preparing for a visit in

Using an **enterprise/action plan** template is ideal for **planning** this activity.

- What does the visitor need to know about your class?
- What do you need to know about the visitor?
- How will the visit be organised?
- What do you hope to learn from the visitor?
- When and how will you evaluate and record the learning?

Tip: Always apply the PEP and articulate skills gained.

Arrange the following for a visit in:

- A suitable room with suitable equipment, e.g. overhead/video/data projector.
- Put a 'do not disturb' notice on the door and switch off the intercom.
- Prepare nametags and a copy of questions/templates.
- Have a camera or camcorder ready, but be sure to get permission from the visitor before using them.

Why have a visitor?

- This is an integral part of the LCVP syllabus – the specific learning outcomes (SLOs): 'Arrange a visitor from a training scheme, community enterprise, voluntary organisation and/or a business enterprise.'
- This activity also enables you to write portfolio items.
- It helps to create awareness of your area and/or organisations.
- It is also good public relations (PR) for the organisation the speaker represents.
- It helps to establish contacts for a work placement or an interview for your career investigation.

Pre-visit in

- Research the speaker and organisation. Hold a class discussion about the proposed visit.
- Brainstorm a list of questions using the specific learning outcomes (SLOs). Don't waste time asking questions if you have already researched the information.
- Assign different responsibilities to each student, e.g. meeting the visitor, introducing the visitor, asking questions, thanking the visitor.
- Arrange the room to suit the activity.
- Ensure that your objectives are SMART (specific, measurable, attainable, realistic in the timeframe).

During the visit

- Be courteous at all times.
- Listen attentively to the visitor.
- Record the main points, perhaps using a template.
- Complete the task assigned and thank the visitor.

Post-visit

- Did the visit go according to plan?
- What worked well?
- How did you all work as a team?
- What would you do differently?
- Did anything go wrong? Why?
- Did you have an individual role?
- Send a thank you, e.g. letter, e-mail, phone call.

Visit Out

Visits out to an enterprise, voluntary organisation and/or training scheme are an extremely effective activity. As with all LCVP activities, you need to be actively involved in the **learning cycle**.

To obtain maximum benefit from the visit, you need maximum preparation.

Pre-visit out

- Decide what business or organisation to visit and gather as much information as possible about it, e.g. search websites, e-mail, telephone or write a letter.
- Obtain permission from the school principal for the visit.
- Contact the business for permission to visit. Give your name, the name of the school, your teacher's name, times, dates and the number of students.
- Agree on a date and time and organise travel arrangements. Ensure all pupils are covered by insurance.
- If costs are involved, collect money from all students.
- Brainstorm a list of questions to ask during the visit.
- Hold a class discussion about the proposed visit and the different tasks each student has, e.g. one person to introduce the group, one person to thank the host.
- Inform your other teachers of the visit. Tell them the date and time.

Visit out

- Be courteous at all times.
- Listen attentively during the visit and ask relevant questions.
- Record main points and observations.
- Complete the task assigned.
- Observe and apply legislation, e.g. health and safety regulations in the workplace.

Post-visit out

- Hold a class discussion about all aspects of the visit.
- Evaluate the visit and discuss different ways to evaluate.
- Ensure a thank you is sent to the business, e.g. e-mail or letter.
- Write a summary report on the visit.
- Note how many specific learning outcomes (SLOs) were achieved.

Cross-curricular – Link the Learning

There are wide ranges of opportunities to develop cross-curricular links. The principal specific learning outcomes (SLOs) that refer to the cross-curricular learning are:

- Link the activities to learning in relevant Leaving Certificate subjects and how they were useful.
- The responsibility for cross-curricular learning is on you. When planning or debriefing at the end of an activity, always ask cross-curricular questions. For example:
  - What Leaving Certificate subjects were useful to me in this activity, in particular my vocational subject groupings (VSGs)?
  - How were these subjects useful?

Linkages between Your Vocational Subject Groupings (VSGs)

For example, a link could be established between Music and Business by having a music-related enterprise activity, such as a concert, and inviting in an entrepreneur who has set up a business associated with music.

Linkages between Your Vocational Subject Groupings and Other Leaving Certificate Subjects

For example, report writing is a skill practised in English and may also be used in Engineering, Construction Studies, Home Economics, Business and the Link Modules.

Linkages between Subjects and the Wider Community (e.g. Work Placements, Visits Out, Career Investigations)

- Many of the specific learning outcomes (SLOs) offer opportunities for linkages. For example:
  - Health and safety: Also important in Chemistry, Home Economics, Construction Studies, Engineering.
  - Teamwork: Used in Chemistry while participating in experiments.
  - Economic activities: Also studied in Economics, Business and Geography.
- Identify links between Leaving Certificate subjects as you participate in Link Module activities.

After each activity, always ask yourself:
- What Leaving Certificate subjects were useful?   • How were they useful?

What Are Your LCVP Skills and Qualities?

As part of the LCVP, you need to be aware of your qualities and skills.

- Learn how to identify your skills and qualities. You need to be able to record them in the curriculum vitae, career investigation, reports and recorded interview. You also need to articulate an understanding of them for the written examination.
- Skills are required for further education, the world of work, being involved in your local community or starting a business.
- A quality is an inherent personal characteristic. For example, one of the most important qualities a nurse can possess is empathy.
- A skill is defined as the learned capacity of a person to carry out an activity with the minimum outlay of time, energy or both. Unlike a quality, a skill is not necessarily inherent but can be acquired.
- It is important to show evidence that you possess a range of skills. Be able to give examples of them as a result of the Link Modules.

Tip: These qualities are explained in the enterprise section.

Qualities

- Determination
- Enthusiasm
- Energy

- Drive
- Honesty
- Being flexible

- Innovative/creative
- Motivator
- Inner control

 Make sure you can describe each one and give an example.

Skills in the Link Modules Classroom

- The first step is to identify skills. You might not be aware of the skills you possess, both individually and as a group.
- You need to be aware of which skills you need to develop.
- When documenting an individual objective for a portfolio item (plans, reports, etc.), make sure it includes three skills, which will create an excellent statement to elaborate on.

Use a Venn diagram (page 202) to compare and contrast skills and qualities.

Sample of Skills and Their Uses in LCVP

Communication skills

- Contacting and making arrangements to invite speakers to the LCVP classroom
- Briefing speakers (e.g. entrepreneurs, volunteers) about the LCVP
- Making presentations in the Link Modules classroom and to outside organisations/agencies
- Sending thank you letters, e-mails, phone calls
- Ensuring other students are interested and involved in activities
- Introducing, listening and summarising Link Modules activities
- Chairing meetings in the LCVP class

Teamwork skills

- Group activities, e.g. team enterprise, 'My Own Place' investigation
- Seeking help when required from the Link Modules teacher and other adults
- Helping others in the LCVP class to achieve their objectives
- Assessing the effectiveness of the team and seeing how it can be improved
- Resolving problem situations: avoid apportioning blame, use negotiation techniques to support others members to learn from mistakes
- Discussion, group disagreements, norming, forming and performing

Revise teamwork on pages 126–7, as a number of activities are team activities.

Organisation skills

- Being able to decide who does what and organising groups
- Setting up the room for the LCVP visitor
- Preparing for your work placement
- Obtaining and collecting permission slips for outside visits
- Making time arrangements and finalising administration and the room
- Organising meetings, visits out and visits in
- Organising an enterprise activity, e.g. a fundraiser

Research skills

- Organising material and designing questionnaires
- Gathering information through questionnaires, interviews and websites
- Reading, summarising and analysing information obtained
- Identifying sources of information, e.g. for your career investigation, identifying pathways
- Analysing information and evaluating

Administrative skills

- Writing letters, e-mails, plans and reports
- Word-processing materials, e.g. letters
- Keeping records of all LCVP activities
- Telephoning, e-mailing, sending thank you cards

Presentation skills

- Structuring material
- Using visual stimuli to enhance presentations
- Deciding on what to say and how to say it
- Arguing and debating points
- Public speaking

Information technology skills

- E-mailing speakers for the LCVP
- Sourcing and using websites to investigate careers, entrepreneurs and the 'My Own Place' report
- Using camera and video, e.g. in the recorded interview
- Word-processing reports and plans
- Editing materials and perfecting portfolio items
- Using computer software, e.g. Excel for accounts
- Acquiring accurate keyboard skills

Analysis skills

- Presenting facts from researching Link Modules
- Preparing summaries, tables and diagrams for LCVP reports
- Understanding material and information
- Solving problems in your own way

Other skills

Sometimes skills can be defined using the following headings.

Technical/ practical skills	Personal skills/ qualities	Interpersonal/ group skills
→ Writing letters/e-mails → Modern European languages → Information technology skills → Researching → Managing finance → Numbers → Idea generation → Designing advertisements/art → Telephone skills → Being good with your hands → Knowledge of materials → Making things → Report writing → Writing enterprise/ action plans	→ Honest → Dependable → Willing to learn → Confident → Determined → Creative → Show initiative → Know your strengths → Humorous → Friendly → Organised → Admit mistakes → Accept criticism → Express your opinion	→ Work well with others → Communicate well → Lead others/ chair meetings → Allow others to lead → Deal with conflict → Listen to others → Teach skills to others → Meet and greet strangers → Seek the opinion of others → Ensure others are heard → Speak in front of a group → Follow the ideas of others → Encourage others → Get on with authority

Post-experience – Evaluation

Every activity needs to be evaluated. Evaluation looks at the relevance, quality, value and usefulness of the activity. Effective evaluation enables successes to be celebrated, areas of difficulty to be pinpointed and plans to be put in place to eliminate known weaknesses. Evaluation is part of the learning cycle for all LCVP activities and usually takes place at the end of an activity.

When you evaluate, you are looking back to see how far the activity went in achieving its objectives.

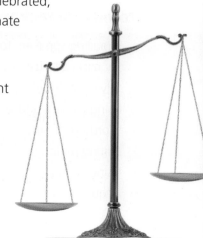

After each LCVP activity, articulate the skills you developed.

Stages of evaluation: DAR

1. **Debriefing: Gather all the information.**
   - What did you learn?
   - What went well?
   - Did you meet your objectives and aims?
2. **Assessing information: Examine and discuss the information.**
   - How useful was the activity?
   - What did not work well?
   - How well did you all work together as a team?
3. **Recommendations: How can you improve for future activities?**

Evaluation should enhance and make sense of the activity. Set aside enough **time** for debriefing and evaluating. You often learn most when responding to an activity. The **s**pecific **l**earning **o**utcomes (SLOs) are worth exploring in evaluation and debriefing sessions.

Why Evaluate?

- Receiving feedback is an important part of any activity.
- Evlauation determines whether or not the activity was worthwhile. Were new skills learned or applied?
- It helps you prepare for future activities and learn from mistakes.
- It determines whether or not you achieved your objectives and aims. Did the activity go according to your plan? This will demonstrate whether or not you were realistic.
- It clarifies any issues and challenges, e.g. time management: were the actual times scheduled adhered to?

How to Evaluate LCVP Activities

Questionnaires

- Questionnaires are easy to prepare.
- It is easy to collate information.
- They are inexpensive to produce. You can have a hard paper copy or use online tools, such as Google forms.
- Replies are confidential.
- There is usually a good response rate.
- Everybody is given the same questions, which ensures accuracy.

Class discussion

- There is no need to prepare, so a class discussion is quick and inexpensive.
- Comments made can be elaborated on, ensuring understanding.
- Students have an opportunity to practise communication skills.
- All students are included.
- Compare this activity to others.

Teacher's/speaker's opinions

- This is an extremely quick way to collate views.
- There are no costs involved.
- Your teacher is a good judge.
- Can comment on a student's individual contribution.
- This method can highlight the differences between this activity and others.

Written report

- This provides you with an opportunity to give individual comments.
- It is easy to see what you have learned.
- It is an ideal opportunity to practise IT skills.
- A written report is also part of the LCVP assessment (both the portfolio and written exam).

Review and evaluation are important at the end of each LCVP activity for the following reasons:

1. Were the aims achieved? Did it go according to how you planned the activity? It shows if the aims were realistic to start off with.
2. Were teachers, speakers, visit out personnel, work placement employers and students satisfied with the activity? If not, why not?
3. Teamwork: It identifies who participated and who needs to contribute more.
4. Cost: It identifies if costs were kept within budget.
5. Time management: Were actions done according to the schedule?
6. It's also important to show what new skills are learned.

Summary Report

Core item (300–600 words)

The summary report in the LCVP is a clear, short and concise written document. The report is based on an LCVP activity and the specific learning outcomes (SLOs) provide you with many possibilities for writing a summary report. The following are some ideas:

- Visitor to the Link Modules classroom, e.g. an entrepreneur
- Visit out as part of the Link Modules, e.g. a visit to a training scheme

Template: Summary Report Based on a Link Modules Activity

Title	The report must have a clearly identifiable title, e.g. 'A summary report on a LCVP visit to Google'.
Author	Your name
Terms of reference OR Aims: **– Group** **– Personal**	Why the report was written or requested OR what you/the group hope to achieve. Have three aims. Make sure one is a personal aim.
Body of the report (at least three paragraphs)	Lay out paragraphs in a logical sequence. Numbered or bold headings and bulleted lists are recommended. Be sure to elaborate, as detail is required. Use a logical sequence – apply the learning cycle (PEP). Remember, you are reporting on the LCVP activity. This is not an essay. Strike a balance between the activity and the content.
Conclusions	Concise list. These should refer back to the aims.
Recommendations	These are suggestions for future action based on the summary report's conclusions. They might also include follow-on activities or describe how you might perform better in a future exercise. Be sure to elaborate.

 Remember, a summary report is written in the past tense.

Ideas for a summary report:
- A visitor to the LCVP classroom
- A visit out to an enterprise

Summary Report Template

Title	
Author	
Aims	
Body of report	
Conclusions	
Recommendations	

> Remember you're reporting on an activity.

All portfolio items must be consistent. See the tips on page 191.

It is not an essay. Make sure to balance reporting on the activity and the content in your report.

Checklist for success criteria for the summary report

When you have finished your summary report, read the list below to make sure you fulfil the LCVP requirements. Be sure to elaborate and articulate each portfolio item. Go to Section 4: Assessment to check general rules for the portfolio and apply the ten tips for perfecting your portfolio items on pages 190–91.

- ✓ Is your summary report word-processed?
- ✓ Did you check that the word count is between 300 and 600 words?
- ✓ Have you checked the layout and presentation against the LCVP guidelines?
- ✓ Have you corrected any spelling, grammar or punctuation errors?
- ✓ Have you been consistent in the use of capital letters, underlining, font, bold, italics and indentation?
- ✓ Does your summary report have a title that tells the reader what the report is about? Does the title relate to an LCVP activity? Is the report on the activity?
- ✓ Did you state your name as the author of the report?
- ✓ Have you set out three aims for the activity you are reporting on?
- ✓ Did you include at least one personal aim as well as group aims?
- ✓ Have you used full sentences?
- ✓ In the body of the report, have you used clear, short, well-structured sentences?
- ✓ Does the content of the report refer to the terms of reference or aims that you set out above?
- ✓ Have you used headings and subheadings where appropriate?
- ✓ Does your report make sense to the reader? (Remember, the reader will not know anything about the activity that you are reporting on, so your description is important.)
- ✓ Are your statements logical?
- ✓ Have you referred to your own involvement in the activity?
- ✓ Did you list three conclusions you have drawn from the activity?
- ✓ Did your conclusions relate to the aims you set out at the beginning of the report?
- ✓ Based on the conclusions you came to, did you make at least two recommendations?
- ✓ Proofread your summary report to make sure it is free of errors and as perfect as possible.

Work in pairs and use this checklist to evaluate your portfolio. Ask for explanations.

Twenty Sample Questions

1. What steps should be taken to ensure that the visit in is organised properly and run efficiently?

2. Explain **three** objectives that the class might have for organising the visit.

3. Name a business or organisation your class has visited as part of the Link Modules. Describe **two** factors that contributed to the success or failure of the visit.

4. Why it is important to evaluate your visit?

5. Describe **three** methods that could be used to evaluate the visit out. Give a reason for choosing each method.

6. Name an organisation you have visited and give a brief outline of the work or service it provides. Outline **two** reasons why you undertook the visit.

7. Write a letter to a friend in London describing what you have learned from an LCVP visit in.

8. Describe **four** ways the local community benefits from a voluntary organisation.

9. Name **three** LC subjects (other than Link Modules) you are studying. Indicate how each was useful in the organisation or planning of a visit in and how this activity helped you in each subject.

10. Why is it important for a business to plan?

11. Under **three** appropriate headings, set out a plan for a business or mini company that has a new product for sale.

12. State **two** uses of a business plan.

13. Consider an enterprise you have been involved in while undertaking the Link Modules. Using appropriate headings, set out a business plan for this enterprise.

14. Why is research important?

15. Draw up the questionnaire you would use to carry out research in your school.

16. What would you need to consider or plan for to ensure the survey is successful?

17. What areas should be examined in evaluating the process?

18. Draft an agenda for a meeting to prepare for a visit out.

19. List questions that could be asked on the visit out.

20. Draft an e-mail to thank the organisation for a visit out.

The aim of this unit is to encourage and facilitate you to find out for yourself as much as possible about **working life** and **local employment opportunities**.

Specific Learning Outcomes (SLOs)

(as listed in the syllabus)

When you have finished working through this unit, you should be able to:

1.1 Identify the main sources of employment in the local area

1.2 Identify the main social services and job creation agencies in the local area

1.3 Identify the main agencies that provide transport in the local area

1.4 Identify the main financial institutions servicing the needs of the local area

1.5 Identify the main agencies involved in industrial relations in the local area

1.6 Identify the principal economic activities in the local area

1.7 Evaluate the potential for tourism in the local area

1.8 Identify and understand the main differences between school and work

1.9 Describe the intrinsic value of various forms of work, including self-employment and voluntary work

1.10 Understand current regulations/legislation relating to the employment of young workers

1.11 Understand current health and safety regulations in workplaces

1.12 Role-play a situation that could give rise to a dispute in the workplace

1.13 Understand issues related to diversity in the workplace

1.14 List the different forms of assistance for unemployed people

1.15 Arrange a visit to a training scheme in the locality and/or invite an appropriate speaker from such an organisation to visit the group in the school

1.16 Link the activities in this unit to learning in relevant Leaving Certificate subjects

KEY WORDS

Skills · Employment · Contract of Employment · Tourism · Responsibilities · Planning · Employment Equality · Economic Activity · Financial Institutions · Diversity · Evaluation · Legislation · Initiatives · Training Scheme · Rights · Industrial Relations · Social Services · Health & Safety

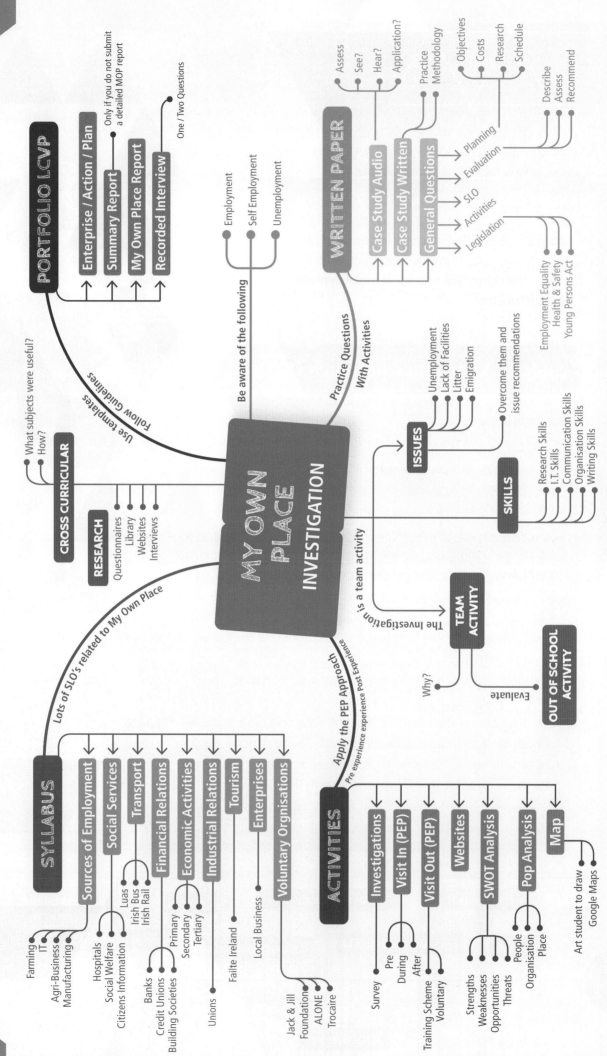

PORTFOLIO LCVP
- Enterprise / Action / Plan
- Summary Report — Only if you do not submit a detailed MOP report
- My Own Place Report
- Recorded Interview — One / Two Questions

CROSS CURRICULAR
- What subjects were useful?
- How?

RESEARCH
- Questionnaires
- Library
- Websites
- Interviews

Use templates
Follow Guidelines

Be aware of the following
- Employment
- Self Employment
- Unemployment

WRITTEN PAPER
- Case Study Audio
  - Assess
  - See?
  - Hear?
  - Application?
- Case Study Written
  - Practice
  - Methodology
- General Questions
  - Objectives
  - Costs
  - Research
  - Schedule

Practice Questions
With Activities

Planning
Evaluation
  - Describe
  - Assess
  - Recommend
SLO
Activities
Legislation
  - Employment Equality
  - Health & Safety
  - Young Persons Act

MY OWN PLACE INVESTIGATION

ISSUES
- Unemployment
- Lack of Facilities
- Litter
- Emigration
- Overcome them and issue recommendations

SKILLS
- Research Skills
- I.T. Skills
- Communication Skills
- Organisation Skills
- Writing Skills

The Investigation is a team activity

TEAM ACTIVITY
- Why?
- Evaluate

OUT OF SCHOOL ACTIVITY

Lots of SLO's related to My Own Place

SYLLABUS
- Sources of Employment
  - Farming
  - IT
  - Agri-Business
  - Manufacturing
- Social Services
  - Hospitals
  - Social Welfare
  - Citizens Information
- Transport
  - Luas
  - Irish Bus
  - Irish Rail
- Financial Relations
  - Banks
  - Credit Unions
  - Building Societies
- Economic Activities
  - Primary
  - Secondary
  - Tertiary
- Industrial Relations
  - Unions
- Tourism
  - Failte Ireland
- Enterprises
  - Local Business
- Voluntary Orgnisations
  - Jack & Jill Foundation
  - ALONE
  - Trocaire

Apply the PEP Approach
Pre experience experience Post Experience

ACTIVITIES
- Investigations
  - Survey
- Visit In (PEP)
  - Pre
  - During
  - After
- Visit Out (PEP)
  - Training Scheme
  - Voluntary
- Websites
- SWOT Analysis
  - Strengths
  - Weaknesses
  - Opportunities
  - Threats
- Pop Analysis
  - People
  - Organisation
  - Place
- Map
  - Art student to draw
  - Google Maps

'My Own Place'

'My Own Place' is an investigation into certain aspects of your local area. Divide the class into groups to investigate voluntary organisations, financial institutions, employment, tourism, social services, job creation agencies, sports facilities, local enterprises and transport.

A 'My Own Place' investigation is an ideal way to achieve the learning outcomes in this unit.

What to Investigate?

Sources of employment

Sources of employment could also be categorised under economic activities and includes:

- Farming
- Agriculture
- Fishing
- Construction
- Manufacturing companies
- IT
- Banks
- Retailers

Make sure you can identify and give examples of the institutions and services in your local area.

Social services

Social services include hospitals, clinics, voluntary organisations (such as Alone), Citizen Information Centres and social welfare offices.

Job creation agencies

- IDA Ireland is the Irish government agency responsible for attracting foreign direct investment. They have attracted successful companies to Ireland, particularly in the IT sector.
- Enterprise Ireland provides support for Irish businesses.
- Other agencies include Leader and Area Partnerships.

These agencies have a significant impact on your area.

Transport

Transport includes airports, train services (Irish Rail, Luas, Dart), haulage companies, buses (e.g. Bus Éireann), taxis and couriers.

Education facilities

- Pre-school
- Primary school
- Post-primary school
- Third level

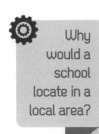
Why would a school locate in a local area?

Financial institutions

These are organisations that provide a range of financial services, including loans.

- Banks, e.g. Bank of Ireland, AIB, Ulster Bank
- Credit unions
- Building societies, e.g. EBS
- Insurance companies, e.g. Aviva

Principal economic activities

Principal economic activities describe the different types of businesses. These can be divided into three categories:

- **Primary:** Agriculture, fishing, forestry and mining
- **Secondary:** Manufacturing and construction
- **Tertiary services:** Financial, retail, transport, legal and medical

Potential for tourism

- Geography features, e.g. sea, lakes, cliffs, mountains
- Historical features, e.g. castles, caves, ancient forts, graveyards
- Services, e.g. hotels, restaurants, guesthouses
- Recreational services, e.g. golf, pitch and putt, gyms, swimming pools, adventure centres
- Transport to facilitate access for tourists

Enterprises in your own area

- Business enterprises
- Voluntary and community enterprises

Use the local enterprise questionnaire on page 146.

When investigating these services, be sure to describe the significance of these agencies or businesses.

- They provide a service.
- They create jobs and employment.
- They offer better facilities in the area.
- They make the area more attractive to live in and for tourists.

Definition of 'My Own Place'

'My Own Place' has a **broad definition** to cater for both urban and rural settings. It can include the following:

- A class survey to decide on 'My Own Place'
- Your route to school (walk, bike, car, bus, Luas, Dart, train) or a street survey
- A suitable local shopping centre, industrial estate or block of shops to survey
- Your local village, town or city

'My Own Place' is quite extensive and may be best achieved by engaging in a **number of investigations** while doing other activities. Use a team approach to generate all the specific learning outcomes (SLOs).

Top Tips for Investigating 'My Own Place'

- Decide on objectives that are specific, measurable, achievable and realistic and give each one a timeframe (SMART).
- Define the area and scope of investigation.
- Sketch a map.
- Research 'My Own Place' using a variety of methods, e.g. questionnaires, interviews, the internet.
- What specific learning outcomes (SLOs) can you achieve?
- Use a team approach and divide up the work.
- Brainstorm possible questions.
- Invite a speaker, e.g. someone who works in planning or a local council representative.
- Do a SWOT analysis (strengths, weaknesses, opportunities and threats).
- Investigate at least one voluntary organisation, community enterprise and business enterprise in detail.
- Arrange a walking tour, if possible, and/or a visit out/visit in.

Tip: Use an enterprise/action plan template to plan 'My Own Place'.
Methodology
Who? How? What? When? Where? Why?

Remember, the report on 'My Own Place' may be based on a single investigation over a short period or on a number of events that take place at intervals over the two years of the Link Module.

Since the 'My Own Place' report assesses a number of skills and information, you may decide to write this detailed report after participating in all the LCVP activities. Activities such as teamwork, researching and investigating will help you prepare this detailed report. Use an enterprise/action plan template to plan this investigation, which ensures a **portfolio item**. Design a questionnaire for 'My Own Place'.

Useful Resources

- Local newspapers and directories
- Internet, e.g. citizens information website
- Fáilte Ireland
- Planning office and chamber of commerce
- Library
- County council
- Subject teachers/students

What challenges might your local area face in the future?

1. Unemployment due to the recession and closure of businesses.
2. Emigration as a result of unemployment.
3. Environmental issues; pollution.

Tip: Discuss how you would overcome these issues.

Introduction to Working Life

Work can be defined as an activity that requires effort, e.g. washing the dishes at home.

Employment is when payment is received for working, e.g. washing dishes in a canteen and getting paid. People in employment are employers, employees or self-employed people.

- Employers are people who hire workers in return for payment.
- Employees are people who work for employers.
- Self-employed people work for themselves.

Tip: List the different types of work you are involved in.

Different Types of Work

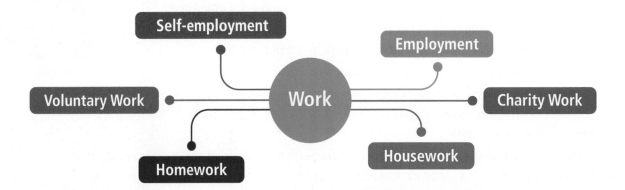

Self-employment · Employment · Voluntary Work · Work · Charity Work · Homework · Housework

School to Work

What are the main differences between work and school?

- **Time:** The hours are longer. You may have to work until 5pm or on weekends.
- **Income:** You get paid for working. You don't get paid for attending school.
- **Practical:** Work is hands on. In school, you spend a lot of time sitting at a desk.
- **Teamwork:** You may have more opportunities to participate in groups compared with school situations.

When leaving school to start your working life, you may encounter **challenges**.

- Time management
- Money management
- New relationships and different roles
- Rights
- Responsibilities
- Freedom and independence

It is important to be aware of local employment opportunities and services and contact details.

Voluntary Work

Many voluntary organisations rely on people to work without pay and help the less well off, e.g. St Vincent De Paul. Voluntary work is very important to our society. You may have the chance to participate as a voluntary worker, which will provide you with many benefits.

Why would you do voluntary work? To improve your self-esteem, help others, acquire new skills, etc.

Music Generation is Ireland's national music education programme. It was initiated by Music Network and funded by U2.

Employment

When you start employment, you may have a full-time or part-time position or you may be employed on a contract basis. As an employee, you may have the opportunity to **job-share** or work **flexitime**. In return for working, you will receive remuneration or payment of some kind. The main form of remuneration is **wages**, which can be paid on the basis of hours worked (**time rate**), units produced (**piece rate**), percentage of sales (**commission**) or a fixed monthly **salary**. You may also receive an additional lump sum (**bonus**) or a percentage of profits (**profit-sharing**). In addition to wages or salaries, you may receive rewards called **benefits-in-kind**, e.g. a company car, special discounts or health insurance payments. There are also non-financial benefits associated with employment, e.g. self-esteem. If an employee is paid a time rate, his or her hours must be monitored.

Permanent full-time work

If you are lucky enough to have a permanent job, there are many advantages and disadvantages.

Advantages	Disadvantages
■ You will have a regular income. ■ You do not have to worry about finding a job. ■ You can join a pension. ■ It is easier to plan your own finances and future. ■ Security of employment gives independence. ■ Promotion prospects exist. ■ You are less likely to become depressed.	■ You have no incentive to move job. ■ Work tends to be less varied. ■ Less leisure and family time is available. ■ You may lose flexibility. ■ Moving house becomes more difficult. ■ Motivation may decrease, as you have the certainty of your job.

Part-time work

With part-time work, you work a minimum of 8 hours per week on a **regular** basis.

Time rate

If an employee is paid a time rate, his or her hours must be monitored. How can timekeeping be monitored?

- Sign an attendance book
- Clock in/clock out cards
- Personal checks
- Video cameras
- Scan in ID cards

Why monitor workers?

- Workers will learn to be punctual.
- Wages can be calculated accurately.
- One can check if employees are reliable.
- A must for flexitime, as employees will have a range of starting times.

Contract of employment

When you are working, you must receive a **contract of employment**. This document sets out all the terms and conditions relating to the position offered. A contract of employment will contain the following information.

Contract of Employment

- Employer's name and address
- Employee's name and address
- Job title
- Job description
- Date of commencement
- Salary
- Holiday entitlements
- Duration of contract and probationary period, if any
- Signature of employee
- Any other conditions appropriate to the job (hours of work, location)
- Pension arrangements

Unemployment

Many people are unable to find suitable employment and are said to be unemployed. This may happen due to business closures, a change in the economy (e.g. a recession) or improvements in technology. When a person is unemployed, they receive unemployment benefit.

If you are unemployed for a time, you should consider it an opportunity to develop new skills. There are many training schemes for the unemployed.

Training Schemes for the Unemployed

Tip: Investigate training schemes for the unemployed.

Solas focuses on planning, funding and driving the development of a learner-focused integrated further education and training service.

Springboard Initiative in higher education offers free part-time courses at certificate, degree and masters level, leading to qualifications that are in demand among employers. Most courses are one year or less in duration, and Springboard is open to job-seekers who have a previous history of employment and believe that a focused, high-quality qualification is the key to getting back to work.

Skillsnets is a state-funded, enterprise-led support body dedicated to the promotion and facilitation of training and up-skilling as key elements in sustaining Ireland's national competitiveness.

Back to Education Allowance (BTEA) Scheme is an educational opportunities scheme for people receiving certain social welfare payments and who want to pursue an approved full-time second- or third-level course (and a limited number of post-graduate courses) of education in an approved college leading to a recognised qualification.

VTOS schemes are run by the Department of Education and Skills and operated through the VECs. Courses must be **full time** and can take as long as two years and lead to qualifications such as Junior Certificate, Leaving Certificate and NFQ certificates. The scheme aims to give **unemployed people** education and training opportunities that will help them find a job and to prepare people to go to paid employment or to further educational opportunities leading to paid employment. If you are registered as unemployed, you **will not** have to sign on at your local social welfare office while on the course.

Youthreach offers a flexible programme of education, vocational training and work experience for 15- to 20-year-olds who have left school early without any formal qualifications.

There are many benefits for unemployed people to engage in further education and training. This also applies to employed people:

- It can improve your skills, therefore creating more opportunities in terms of keeping your job and improving your promotion prospects.
- Certain careers are changing at a rapid rate and need constant up-skilling, e.g. the constant new developments in the IT sector.
- With a change in career and job opportunities, it would be important to continually up-skill. It will also help you find work, enhance your CV and open up more employment prospects.
- It keeps workers motivated and able to deal with new challenges.

What options are available if you become unemployed and want to return to work?

- Retrain by participating in different courses, such as VTOs.
- Set up your own business. Be sure to get advice from mentors.
- Participate in voluntary work, which will help up-skill and improve your CV.
- Work part time and avail of other opportunities, such as a part-time course.
- Avail of opportunities in other countries. Some countries issue work permits to overcome shortages in their labour market.
- Make sure your information is up to date. Log on to The Department of Social Protection's website.

Remember, employment is not all about financial benefits. There are many non-financial benefits too.

However, setting up an enterprise in your area may have challenges.

- People may have less money as a result of unemployment or recession. You can overcome this by selling cheaper products, offering credit and using loyalty cards.
- The population may be decreasing due to emigration. One idea may be to organise festivals, such as The Gathering.

The Future of Work

The future of work is difficult to predict. Many changes are possible as a result of changes in the global economy, competition, changes in technology and also in our own economy. Employees will need to be flexible and adaptable. Meeting the ever-changing demands of the workplace will be a lifelong challenge.

Changes in Employment

- Employees will change jobs and careers many times during their working life.
- More people will work from home.
- Changes in technology mean the types of jobs available are changing continuously.
- More people are working part time, flexitime or job-sharing.
- More people are opting for self-employment.
- More people are working in services and trades.
- There are changes in economic activities.

> A job for life is a thing of the past. Careers for life are an exception rather than the rule.

Rights and Responsibilities

Employees' Rights

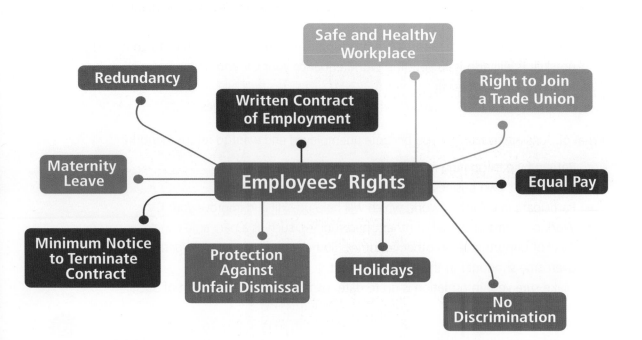

Employees' Responsibilities

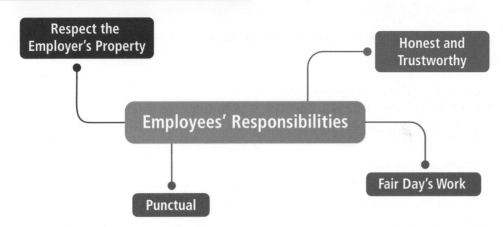

Respect the Employer's Property

Honest and Trustworthy

Employees' Responsibilities

Punctual

Fair Day's Work

Discuss the above rights and responsibilities of an employee. We are often aware of our **rights**, but we must not forget our **responsibilities** and obligations.

What is the minimum wage?

Employers' Responsibilities

Pay the Minimum Wage

Provide a Written Contract

Obey Laws

Employers' Responsibilities

Do Not Discriminate

Keep Proper Records e.g. PAYE, PRSI

Holidays

Provide a Safe and Healthy Workplace

Employers' Rights

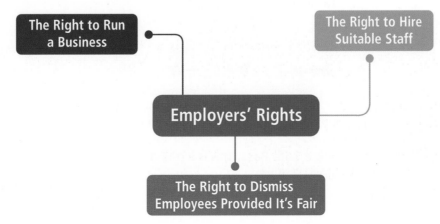

The Right to Run a Business

The Right to Hire Suitable Staff

Employers' Rights

The Right to Dismiss Employees Provided It's Fair

Health and Safety Regulations in the Workplace

Safety, Health and Welfare at Work Act 1993

The Health and Safety Authority (HSA) is responsible for enforcing the Safety, Health and Welfare at Work Act 1993. The HSA, a state-sponsored body, also promotes good standards and provides advice, research and information on health and safety in the workplace. They are responsible for developing and promoting new laws and standards. They may inspect workplaces and investigate any accidents.

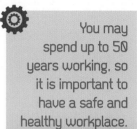

You may spend up to 50 years working, so it is important to have a safe and healthy workplace.

Safety, health and welfare are the responsibility of **both** the employer and the employee.

Employers' obligations

- To provide safe working conditions for all employees. Safety signs should be clearly visible, a Safety Officer should be appointed and appropriate breaks for staff arranged.
- To prepare a Safety Statement outlining hazards and how they can be overcome, eliminated or reduced.
- To provide safe and protective clothing, footwear and equipment as required, e.g. providing safe computer monitors in offices and hard hats on construction sites.
- To provide safety training, information and instructions where necessary and make employees aware of dangers, e.g. train them in safety procedures in the use of certain machines and what to do in the event of a fire.
- To have an anti-bullying policy.
- To facilitate the appointment of an employee as a Health and Safety Representative.

Employees' responsibilities

- To take responsibility for their own safety, health and welfare.
- To use personal protective equipment (PPE) and protective clothing, if required.
- To follow training and instructions carefully.
- To report any dangers or injuries to the Health and Safety Representative or the employer.
- To ensure there is no bullying in the workplace.

Employees must report any hazards!

A **Safety Statement** is a written document identifying hazards and assessing their risk and how to make changes to ensure the workplace is safe. A Safety Statement is required by law. The statement is a declaration in writing of an employer's commitment to safety and health and how to achieve and maintain these standards.

All construction workers must have a **Safe Pass**. This is a one-day course. Everyone on a construction site must have a Safe Pass. If you wish to participate in a work placement on a construction site, you must have a Safe Pass.

You must understand current health and safety regulations in the workplace and be able to follow a set of instructions relating to health and safety.

The objective of the legislation is to prevent accidents and ill health in the workplace. Employers must carry out a hazard list. Once these hazards have been identified, they must state what precautions have been taken and erect warning signs. Safety should be everyone's concern: employers, employees, visitors, etc.

Some of the main **causes of accidents** are:

- Lack of training
- Untidy or cluttered areas
- Not following safety procedures
- Not wearing protective clothing
- Lack of concentration
- Not using machinery correctly
- Haste
- Horseplay

 Smoking in the workplace has been banned since March 2004.

Activity

Complete a health and safety audit of hazards in your school.

Diversity in the Workplace

The workforce in Ireland has changed dramatically. There is a large mix of people working: male, female, young, old, people from different countries, able-bodied people and people with special needs.

The equality legislation in Ireland is not only concerned with gender equality. The **Employment Equality Act 1998–2004** outlines and outlaws discrimination on nine grounds:

- Age
- Gender
- Marital status
- Family status
- Religion
- Race
- Sexual orientation
- Membership of the Traveller community
- Disability

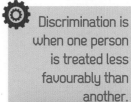 Discrimination is when one person is treated less favourably than another.

It is against the law to discriminate in the following areas:

- Recruitment
- Training
- Promotion
- Dismissals
- Conditions of employment

The Act also **outlines** and **outlaws** the following in the workplace:

- Harassment
- Sexual harassment
- Bullying

Companies must value and promote **equality** and **diversity**. All employees are entitled to equal pay for equal work. The **Equality Authority** was established under this Act and replaced the Employment Equality Agency. The Act also appointed a **Director of Equality Investigations** to investigate complaints of inequality under the Act.

 Harassment is any act or conduct that is offensive, humiliating or intimidating.

Employers are encouraged to put measures in place to promote equality of opportunities. Gender stereotyping involves the assumption that certain jobs are men's jobs and certain jobs are women's.

Diversity in the workplace has many benefits.

- Younger employees can learn from older employees, while older employees can learn new techniques and keep up to date.
- Employees come from many different backgrounds, so they will have a different outlook, which may help in decision-making. This may also create work contacts, which may help your employment prospects in other countries.
- You learn to be tolerant and that we are all the same, regardless of gender, race, ability, etc.
- Different work attitudes will have a positive effect on others.
- Diversity improves a variety of skills, e.g. languages and job prospects.

Young People and Work

Young people have rights and should not be exploited. Both young people and employers should be aware of the Protection of Young Persons (Employment) Act 1996.

The Protection of Young Persons (Employment) Act 1996

Employers' duties

Employers must:

- See a copy of the birth certificate before employing someone under 16 and get the written permission of the parent or guardian.
- Keep a register containing the following details of each person employed who is under 18:
  - Full name
  - Date of birth
  - The time work begins each day
  - The time work ends each day
  - Rates of wages or salary
  - Total amount of wages or salary

Age limit for a regular job

For a regular job, the minimum age is **16**. For light work, employers can hire 14- and 15-year-olds. For example:

This Act protects young workers' health and ensures that work does not put a young person's education at risk.

- Part-time work (legal at 15 years only)
- As part of work experience or an educational programme
- During the school holidays, provided there is a minimum three-week break from work in the summer

Any child under 16 may be employed in film, theatre, sports or advertising under licence.

Maximum hours of work per week

Under-18s may not be employed for more than **40** hours a week or **8** hours a day, except in a genuine emergency.

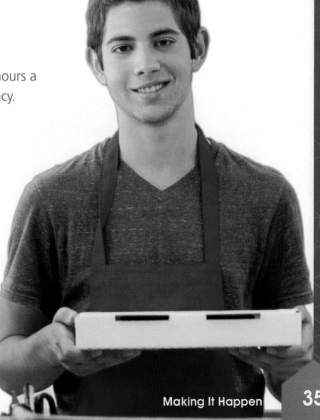

Maximum weekly working hours		
	14 years	**15 years**
Term time	0	8 hours
Holiday work	35 hours	35 hours
Work experience	40 hours	40 hours
Early morning and night work		
Early morning	After 8am	After 6am
Night work with school the next morning	Up to 8pm	Up to 10pm
No school the next morning	Up to 8pm	Up to 10pm and not before 7am
Rest breaks		
30 minutes' break after working	4 hours	$4\frac{1}{2}$ hours
Every 24 hours	14 hours off	12 hours off
Every 7 days	2 days off	2 days off

Exceptions	Penalties
▪ Work at sea ▪ Defence forces ▪ Close relatives (family business or farm)	▪ Offenders could face fines up to €1,904.61 and an extra €317.43 a day for a continuing offence

Industrial Relations

These are the relationships between employers and employees. It is important to develop and maintain good industrial relations in the workplace. Many organisations promote good industrial relations, e.g. trade unions.

Trade Unions

Trade unions are organisations that aim to protect and represent workers in order to improve the conditions of their work. Examples include:

- SIPTU
- Impact
- TUI
- ASTI

Functions of a trade union

1. They represent the interests of workers in the workplace.
2. They negotiate for better wages.
3. They negotiate for upgraded and improved working conditions, such as:
   - Holidays
   - Hours of work
   - Proper facilities in the workplace, e.g. safe clothing and safety equipment
4. They negotiate on behalf of members when there are disputes with employers. The trade union will represent employees in these negotiations.
5. They provide grants for education.
6. They support and promote equality in the workplace by ensuring:
   - All employees are treated equally.
   - Employers obey all the equality legislation.
7. They give workers greater strength by acting together as one.

Every employee has a legal right to join a trade union

Shop steward

- The shop steward is elected by workers to act as their union representative in the workplace.
- He or she recruits new members to the union.
- The shop steward keeps members informed of any union developments.
- He or she represents workers in discussions with management.
- The shop steward acts as a link between the union head office and the workplace.

Irish Business and Employers' Confederation (IBEC)

IBEC is an organisation that represents employers and businesses.

Conflict

Conflict is a disagreement, a struggle or perhaps a fight. Why do people disagree?

- They see things differently.
- They want different things.
- Certain personalities clash.

If an issue arises and causes conflict it must be resolved, otherwise a dispute may result. Conflict may be solved by non-legislative or legislative methods.

There are many mechanisms and institutions to resolve disputes:

- Labour Relations Commission
- Rights Commissioner
- Equality Officer
- Labour Court

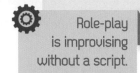
Role-play is improvising without a script.

Role-play

Role-play a situation that could give rise to a dispute in the workplace. Before you start the role-play, you need to be aware of situations that give rise to a dispute.

Rules for role-play:

- Set objectives
- Everyone must have a role
- No bad language
- No bullying
- No inappropriate personal disclosures

Role-play works well for practising conflict resolution or interviews.

After the role-play, allow time for **debriefing and evaluating**. The real value of role-play is in the debriefing. You must document what you learned. It is an excellent way to develop skills, such as communication skills, observation skills and interpersonal skills.

Debriefing

After a role-play, you should document the following.

- What happened?
- Link with previous learning.
- What skills did you use or learn?
- What knowledge did you gain?
- What Leaving Certificate subjects were useful?
- List conclusions.

You are encouraged to role-play a situation that could give rise to a dispute in the workplace.

List some specific learning outcomes (SLOs) that may be achieved through role-play.

To demonstrate your learning, you may decide to submit a detailed 'My Own Place' report or a summary report instead.

Tip:
1,000–1,500 words

Guidelines for the 'My Own Place' Report

Title page	**Title:** This should clearly state that the document is a report on 'My Own Place' and identify the local area being investigated.
	Subtitle: May be added to give more detail about your own area.
	Author's name: Student's name.
	Intended audience: For the attention of the Link Modules teacher.
	Date: Date of completion of the investigation. Always include the year, e.g. 20 January 2017.
Table of contents	This is a list of the main elements of the report, giving the page numbers they appear on. All pages must be numbered and accurate.
Introduction	This should contain a brief description of the local area and indicate the scope of the investigation (i.e. what aspects of the local area are being investigated, as different groups may investigate different areas, e.g. transport, tourism).
	It is a good idea to include a map. Perhaps sketch a map showing the geographical location of the local area or use Google Maps.
Aims/objectives	What you set out to investigate and/or hoped to achieve through the activity. A numbered or bulleted list is acceptable.
	Five objectives are required.
	A personal objective ensures the report is personalised.
	Make sure you include a skills objective (perhaps three skills).
	Group objectives are also acceptable.
Research methods	A concise description of the different ways you or the group organised the collection of relevant information about the local area.
	Short numbered or bulleted sentences are sufficient.
	Include three research methods (make sure they are all different).
	It is a good idea to include one personalised research method.
Out-of-school activity	Record the date, including the year of the activity. Briefly describe what took place and indicate how the information gained was subsequently used.
	This must be a group activity.
Body of the report	**Findings:** This includes the main findings of the investigation. Key aspects of the investigation are described and analysed. Use headings and elaborate on each point.

All portfolio items must be consistent. See the tips on page 191.

Body of the report (continued)	Arrange paragraphs in a logical sequence under clear headings and sub-headings, as appropriate. Small, relevant illustrations, such as maps or statistical tables, may be included here. **Analysis of a local issue:** Identify and analyse an issue relevant to the local area being investigated and propose recommendations. An issue may be a lack of sporting facilities. **Link the learning:** Link the learning to at least two different Leaving Certificate subjects along with an explanation of their relevance. **Personal contribution:** You can document your personal contribution in one of three ways: 1. Include a paragraph entitled 'My Personal Contribution' in the body of the report. This is probably the easiest option. 2. Highlight the personal contribution (e.g. by using *italics*) at appropriate points. 3. Alternatively, you can highlight the personal contribution by including an overview and evaluation of the personal contribution at the end.
Conclusions	Relate the conclusions to the five aims/objectives of the investigation and always elaborate. Link aim 1 to conclusion 1, etc.
Recommendations	Based on the report's conclusions (e.g. suggestions for future action), present three recommendations and be sure to elaborate.
Evaluation	Should include an evaluation of the following: ■ The 'My Own Place' investigation itself ■ The group activity: working in teams ■ Personal performance (if not dealt with separately)
Appendices	Maximum two items, such as photographs, maps, charts or diagrams. Make sure to cross-reference in the main report (e.g. Appendix 1).

Revise the ten tips for perfecting your portfolio on pages 190–91.

'My Own Place' Report Template

Make sure all of the following are included in your 'My Own Place' report.

Title
Subtitle
Author's name
For the attention of
Date (including the year)
Table of contents
Introduction
Aims/objectives (at least five; make sure you include a skills objective)
Research methods
Out-of-school activity
Main findings (could include a graph or chart)
Local issue
Link the learning
Your personal contribution
Conclusions
Recommendations
Evaluation – Of the investigation – Of the group performance
Appendices (maximum of two)

You may decide to write a summary report on 'My Own Place'. If you do this, you cannot submit a detailed report on 'My Own Place'.

All portfolio items must be consistent. See the tips on page 191.

Checklist for success criteria for 'My Own Place' report

When you have finished your 'My Own Place' report, read the list below to make sure you fulfil the LCVP requirements. Be sure to elaborate and articulate the learning for each portfolio item. Go to Section 4: Assessment to check general rules for the portfolio and apply the ten tips for perfecting your portfolio items on pages 190–91.

- ✓ Is your 'My Own Place' report word-processed?
- ✓ Is the report between 1,000 and 1,500 words?
- ✓ Does your 'My Own Place' report relate to an LCVP investigation that you took part in during the course of the two-year programme?
- ✓ Have you been consistent in your use of punctuation, capitals, font, underlining, etc.?
- ✓ Do you have a clear title and subtitle stating it is a report on 'My Own Place'?
- ✓ Did you state your name as the author?
- ✓ Have you included who the report is for the attention of, whom it is for and the date of completion (including the year)?
- ✓ Have you included the table of contents and page numbers?
- ✓ Have you included an introduction describing the area?
- ✓ Does your introduction include the scope of the investigation and a map?
- ✓ Have you stated the group's aims?
- ✓ Have you stated your personal aims, with three skills?
- ✓ Have you described your key aspects?
- ✓ Have you arranged the report in a logical sequence and covered all the requirements?
- ✓ Have you included at least two illustrations or tables?
- ✓ Have you included three different types of research methods?
- ✓ Did you include an out-of-school activity, e.g. a walking tour?
- ✓ Have you dated (including the year) and described the activity?
- ✓ Have you analysed a local issue and issued recommendations to solve the issues?
- ✓ Have you linked the learning to two Leaving Certificate subjects and stated how they were useful?
- ✓ Have you described your personal contribution to this investigation?
- ✓ Did you give at least three conclusions you have drawn from this investigation?
- ✓ Did you relate your conclusions to each of your aims? Are they clear?
- ✓ Are your recommendations based on your conclusions?
- ✓ Have you evaluated the experience of the investigation?
- ✓ Have you evaluated the group/team performance of the investigation?
- ✓ Have you evaluated your individual performance of the investigation?
- ✓ Did you submit an appendix with a maximum of two items? Did you cross-reference them?
- ✓ Proofread your 'My Own Place' report to make sure it is free of errors and as perfect as possible.

Work in pairs and use this checklist to evaluate your portfolio. Ask for explanations.

Mind Map: Outline of a 'My Own Place' Report

AIMS/ OBJECTIVES

Aims (5)
Ensure a skills aim
Group '?'

LOCAL ISSUES
Litter/Traffic/
Sports
Facilities
· Description
· Analysis
· Suggestions

INTRODUCTION
· We/I will investigate
· Scope/aspects
· Map of 'My Own Place'

RESEARCH
Desk/Field

· Internet
· Library
· Questionnaire
· Visitor
· Others

TITLE PAGE
· My own place is ...
· Title/subtitle
· Author, who it is for, date
· Table of contents
· Number of pages

OUT-OF-SCHOOL ACTIVITY
· Date
· What took place?
· How was information used?

START

END

MY OWN PLACE

APPENDICES
· Maximum two items
· Be sure to cross-reference

LEAVING CERTIFICATE SUBJECTS
· At least two subjects
· List
· How were they useful?
· Mention your VSG subjects

EVALUATIONS
(A) Activity and investigation – did you achieve your aims?
(B) Group performance

RECOMMENDATIONS

· Link to conclusions

MY PERSONAL CONTRIBUTION
· One paragraph in body of report OR
· In italics throughout the report OR
· Included in the evaluation

CONCLUSION
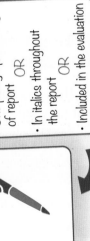
· Link to aims

Learning Board

Key Questions

Answer these questions in your LCVP folder or copybook.

1. Briefly summarise the main points using key words from the unit.
2. Write down something you learned.
3. Write down something you found difficult or challenging.

Devise an Exam Question

Write three exam questions in your LCVP folder or copybook. Start with a quotation, perhaps a specific learning outcome (SLO) or a sentence from this unit.

Presentation

Write a **six-sentence presentation** on the rights and responsibilities of an employee. This can be an individual attempt or work in teams to create a presentation.

Portfolio

Can I use this for my **portfolio**?   Yes ☐   No ☐
The portfolio is worth 60%.

If yes:

CORE – submit all 4

+ Curriculum vitae
+ Enterprise/action plan
+ Career investigation
+ Summary report

OPTIONAL – submit 2 out of 4

+ Diary of work experience
+ Enterprise report
+ Report on 'My Own Place'
+ Recorded interview/presentation

A total of six portfolio items must be submitted.

Skills

Now that you have worked through this unit, what are the next steps?
What new skills have you acquired? Describe them.

Tasks

1. Draft a contract of employment for a job of your choice.
2. Write a brief account of a training scheme.
3. Discuss financial benefits available to unemployed people.
4. Describe the various laws you studied in this unit.
5. Did you discover any useful websites/YouTube clips?

Learning Board

Tip: Revisit after completing all units.

Cross-curricular

Cross-curricular refers to activities or themes that are relevant to many subjects across the curriculum. For example, health and safety is important in Chemistry, Construction Studies, Engineering, Home Economics and Business.

Answer the following in your LCVP folder or copybook.

1. What Leaving Certificate subjects were useful?
2. How were they useful?
3. Were your vocational subject groupings (VSGs) useful?

Learning Outcomes

Revisit the specific learning outcomes on page 21.
Do you understand each SLO?

Key Words

Do you understand the key words on page 21? Write three sentences on each word.

Key Examination Words

Do you understand the key examination words on page 208? For all the main themes, you will need to demonstrate a deep understanding by:

- Describing the term
- Explaining the term
- Demonstrating the term
- Illustrating the term
- Differentiating the term
- Evaluating the term

Tip: This links with Bloom's taxonomy.

Evidence

Tip: Draft a mind map to demonstrate learning in this unit.

You will need to show evidence of your learning. It is your responsibility to keep draft copies of your work. It is a good idea to label and date all activities and handouts in your copy or LCVP folder.

Twenty Sample Questions

Tip: To improve your examination performance, you need to practise.

The questions on page 47 can first be attempted orally, followed by written answers.

Making It Happen: Preparing for Assessment

Assessment ideas based on Preparation for the World of Work
Unit 1 – Introduction to Working Life

Portfolio of coursework – 60%

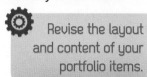

Core

→ **Enterprise/action plan**
1. Plan a 'My Own Place' investigation
2. Plan a visit to a training scheme
3. Invite a visitor to the classroom

→ **Summary report**
1. 'My Own Place' (provided you don't submit a 'My Own Place' report as an optional item)
2. Visit in/visit out to a training scheme

Options

→ **Report on 'My Own Place'**
→ **Recorded interview/presentation**
   – General interview: one or two questions on 'My Own Place'

Revise the layout and content of your portfolio items.

Written paper – 40%

→ **SLOs 1.8 to 1.14 provide many opportunities to be assessed in the written examination:**
   – Differences between school and work, self-employment and voluntary work
   – Legislation: equality, young people and safety, health and welfare
   – Disputes and diversity in the workplace
   – Assistance for the unemployed
   – Training schemes in the locality

→ **Other aspects of 'My Own Place':**
   – Sources of employment, social services, job creation, transport, financial institutions, industrial relations, economic activities and potential for tourism

→ **Questions** that demonstrate that you have participated in an activity. PEP approach (pre-experience, experience, post-experience). Part of the learning cycle of LCVP is planning, participating and evaluating.

→ **Cross-curricular learning** – what Leaving Certificate subjects were useful and how? Refer in particular to your vocational subject groupings (VSGs).

→ **Analyse** your individual contribution and personal performance.

→ **Evaluation:**
   – How and why do we evaluate?
   – Evaluate the 'My Own Place' investigation.
   – Evaluate team performance.

Twenty Sample Questions

1. Consider the area where you live. Give **one** reason why you think your school is located where it is.

Tip: In the examination, a question will normally have four parts. Revise examination preparation.

2. Name **two** types of enterprises or organisations in your area. Explain **one** advantage of each to the area.

3. Identify **two** challenges faced by enterprises or organisations in your area. Explain **two** ways each challenge can be overcome.

4. Explain diversity in the workplace and explain the benefits it might bring to the workplace.

5. What advice would you give to an entrepreneur who is researching the possibility of setting up a business in your area?

6. Name **one** agency or business involved in each of the following: (a) job creation (b) financial services (c) transport services. Describe the significance of this agency or business to the area.

7. Prepare a questionnaire you would use to do an investigation of your local area.

8. What challenges might your local area face over the next five years? Suggest how these might be overcome.

9. Name a voluntary organisation or community enterprise in your local area.

10. Identify and describe a community need not currently being met locally. What suggestions would you make to address that need?

11. Discuss the potential for tourism in your area.

12. Discuss the legislation you studied as part of the LCVP relating to health and safety, employment equality and the Protection of Young Persons (Employment) Act 1996.

13. Choose a local training scheme and discuss how it impacts on the unemployed.

14. What benefits are available for the unemployed?

15. Discuss industrial relations and the functions of trade unions.

16. Discuss a situation that may cause conflict in the workplace.

17. Discuss the rights and responsibilities of employers.

18. Discuss the rights and responsibilities of employees.

19. List **three** types of research to source information on the 'My Own Place' investigation.

20. Discuss the financial benefits and non-financial benefits of being (a) an employee and (b) self-employed.

Tip: Skim Section 4: Assessment, in particular the section on revising exam questions (pages 202–205).

The aim of this unit is to equip you with the skills and confidence necessary to gain employment and to develop your organisational and communicative skills. The involvement of adults from business and the local community is recommended in order to help you practise presenting yourself to prospective employers.

Specific Learning Outcomes (SLOs)

(as listed in the syllabus)

When you have finished working through this unit, you should be able to:

2.1 Recognise the different ways in which job vacancies are advertised

2.2 Apply for a job by letter, telephone and e-mail

2.3 Complete an application form

2.4 Compile and create a curriculum vitae in word-processed format

2.5 Explain how to prepare for a job interview

2.6 Engage in a simulated job interview

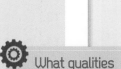

What qualities do I have?

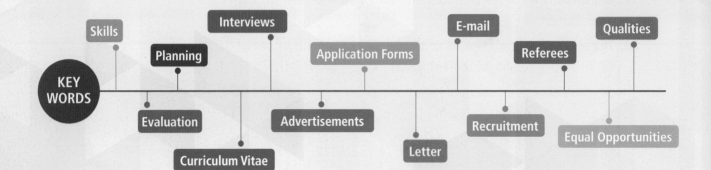

KEY WORDS

Skills · Interviews · Planning · Application Forms · E-mail · Qualities · Referees · Evaluation · Advertisements · Recruitment · Equal Opportunities · Curriculum Vitae · Letter

Work is an integral part of our lives and everyone is seeking the ideal type of work. Work can be paid or unpaid, but there are many benefits:

- Wages are received for paid work.
- Your self-esteem rises and you get a sense of achievement when you do something worthwhile.
- There is the possibility of promotion if you work hard.
- Employees have a chance to improve their skills.
- Opportunities to travel can arise.

There are certain qualities that help make a person more employable:

- **Energy, drive and hard work:** When employees show interest and overcome difficulties.
- **Reliability:** When employees can be trusted and depended on.
- **Enthusiasm and commitment:** When employees show interest, eagerness, dedication and responsibility.
- **Adaptability:** When employees are flexible and can accept change.
- **Good education:** When employees have qualifications and experience.

Selecting and retaining the right staff are critical to a business's success.

Recruitment

Recruitment is more than just placing an advertisement and interviewing. It starts with deciding how to recruit (using an agency, recruiting via newspapers or websites), writing job descriptions and application forms, assessing curriculum vitaes, shortlisting candidates, interviewing, selecting candidates and checking references.

What Ways Can an Employer Use to Recruit?

- Employers can advertise in national or local newspapers (some newspapers have websites) or on television or radio. They can also use the internet or notice boards.
- They can use a recruitment agency.
- They can hire someone who has done work experience with them.
- They can use their contacts to network for the right person.
- They can organise recruitment exhibitions, job fairs or recruitment days.
- They can approach job-training agencies.
- They can hope that word will spread that they are looking for somebody (word of mouth).

Reasons for Job Vacancies

- The business could be expanding and needs more staff.
- Employees could be of retirement age or taking early retirement.
- Employees could be leaving, either to emigrate or work elsewhere.
- The company may need to replace employees on a temporary basis due to illness, maternity leave, career breaks, job-sharing, dismissals, etc.
- Seasonal work may be available, e.g. the tourism industry in the summer months.

Difficulties for Employers When Recruiting

Sometimes it can be difficult to fill a position. This can happen for a variety of reasons:

- The work itself may be boring.
- There may be a skills shortage in that field, e.g. high-tech skills jobs.
- General economic conditions may make it difficult to recruit.
- The location of the business may make it awkward for employees to get to work.
- Wages and working conditions may not be attractive.

Ways to overcome recruitment problems

- Recruit from abroad.
- Offer part-time work, job-sharing and flexitime.
- Provide training opportunities and grants for further education.
- Provide accommodation.
- Link up with local schools and colleges.

What to Do If You Can't Find a Job in Your Chosen Career

- Look for work experience. This will normally be unpaid, but it shows that you have an interest in that job and you will get experience.
- Do some voluntary work.
- Develop skills that are transferable to another job, such as ICT skills.
- Investigate additional courses or qualifications. Or you could retrain and find a career where there are positions.
- Start your own business.
- Emigrate.

 The same options are available if you become unemployed.

Recruitment Agencies

The success of any business depends on its people.
Using a recruitment agency can help a business to find the
ideal employees.

Benefits of using recruitment agencies

- Recruitment agencies offer a full range of services, such as advertising, profiling, interviewing, selecting employees, checking references and, if required, drawing up contracts of employment. This can save time and money.
- Good recruitment agencies attract good applicants.
- Agencies have specialised staff that will recruit more objectively.

Applying for a Job

Usually a candidate will apply for a job using one or more of the following:

- Letter
- Telephone
- E-mail
- Application form
- Curriculum vitae
- Online

Advertisement

Campbell Communications is looking for dynamic salespeople to join its sales team. Campbell Communications is one of the most prestigious mobile distributors.

The successful candidates must have:

- Excellent IT skills
- Excellent communications and interpersonal skills
- Good team skills

For application form and further information,
contact **Campbell Communications** at
1399 The Mall, Athlone.
Telephone 0906 3425157 E-mail: cc@eircom.net

Using adverts you have sourced from local newspapers or using the Campbell Communications advert, answer the following in your LCVP folder or copybook.
- What job is being advertised?
- Who is advertising?
- Where was it advertised?

Equal Opportunities Employer

This means that the employer follows the employment equality legislation (see pages 33–4). Therefore, the employer does not discriminate on the grounds of sex, age, race, religion, gender, ethnic group, marital status or disability. This means that everyone applying for the position has an equal chance.

References

References are used to check the reliability of the applicant. References describe the applicant's qualities and characteristics and indicate if the applicant is suitable for the position. They also verify that all details are correct.

Always ask permission first to make sure you can use someone as a reference.

Applying for a Job by Phone

An advertisement may ask you to telephone for an application form or to arrange an appointment, which may turn into a short telephone interview. Therefore, before you telephone, make sure you're prepared.

Pre-telephoning

- Have the advertisement and your CV in front of you.
- Ideally you should phone from a landline in a quiet room, rather than from a mobile phone or public phone.
- Have a pen and paper ready to record necessary information.
- Check the times and dates when you are available for interview.

During telephoning

- Speak clearly, confidently and slowly, giving your name and your reason for calling.
- Ask to speak to the person whose contact details were given in the advertisement.
- Write down relevant information.
- Listen attentively to questions and ask to have them repeated if you don't understand them.
- If left waiting, remain calm.
- Keep the conversation short.
- Thank the speaker for his or her time.

Post-telephoning

- Reread your notes and make sure you understand what was said.
- Write down the date and the name of the person you spoke to.
- Record the time and date of the interview in your diary.

Sometimes you may reach an answering machine, so prepare a short, clear message with your name and contact details in advance.

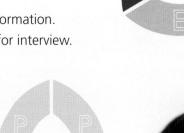

E-mail

E-mail should only be used if stated in the advertisement.

E-mail

To: mobrien@vey.ie
From: michaelomalley@99.ie
Subject: Job Interview
Attachment: Curriculum Vitae

Dear Sir/Madam,
I wish to apply for the position of salesperson as advertised in the
Galway Examiner on Friday, 6 March 2015.

I have excellent skills and qualities, which are suitable for this position.

I am attaching my curriculum vitae.

I look forward to hearing from you.

Yours faithfully,
Michael O'Malley

Jobs can be advertised in many ways, e.g. internet/websites, recruitment agencies and fairs, notice boards, radio, TV and magazines.

Letter of Application

The purpose of a letter of application is to introduce you to a prospective employer and hopefully get an interview. Remember, it will be your first contact with the company and should be of the highest standard in order to create a good impression of you prior to reading your CV or application form.

The letter should highlight the most important points of your CV, in particular your strengths, suitability and why you are applying for this position.

Tips for letter writing

- Letters should be typed, unless the advert specifically asks for handwritten letters.
- Use high-quality, clean, white A4 paper.
- Use black ink.
- Do not use Tipp-Ex.
- Do not send a photocopy.
- Keep words, sentences and paragraphs short.
- Use Times New Roman font and always do a spell-check.

Layout of a letter

1. **Address of the person writing the letter:** Your address and telephone number should be in the top right-hand corner of the page. Check punctuation and give your area code. Leave a gap.

2. **Date:** Include the date, e.g. 12 September 2015.

3. **Name and address of recipient:** This appears on the left-hand side of the page.

4. **Subject line:** This is the purpose of the letter, e.g. Re: Application for Store Manager.

5. **Salutation:** Address the person you are writing to, e.g. *Dear Mrs Josephine Togher.*

6. The **body** of the letter.

    (a) **Beginning:** Introduce yourself and refer to the name and date of the advertisement.

    (b) **Middle:** State your skills, qualities and experience and explain your interest in the job.

    (c) **End:** The closing should be positive and confident. Mention the dates and times that you are available for interview and say that you are looking forward to hearing from him or her.

7. **Complementary close:** If you open with *Dear Sir/Madam*, close with *Yours faithfully.* If you know the name of the person and open with it (e.g. *Dear Mrs Togher*), close with *Yours sincerely.*

8. Insert a line break, followed by your **signature**.

9. Type **your name and title** (Mr, Mrs, Ms).

10. **Enclose:** Mention anything you are sending with the letter, e.g. a curriculum vitae, a reference.

> If you are asked to write a letter in the written exam, you must use a **formal layout** and apply any **relevant text** given in the exam question. Be sure to mention the LCVP or Link Modules too.

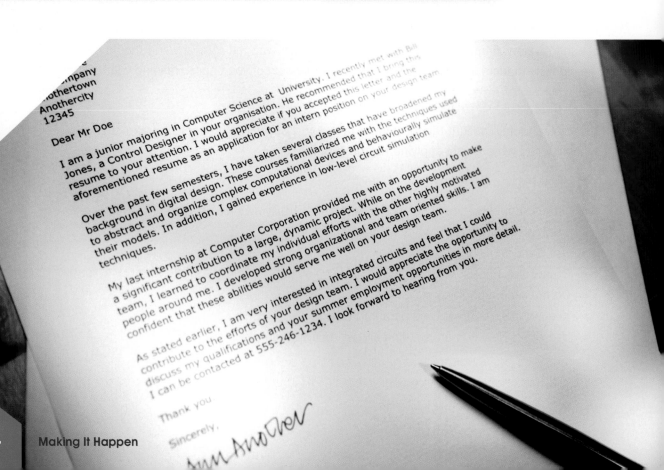

Sample letter layout

Tip: Layout and neatness are important.

1	Address of sender
	_____
	_____
	_____
	_____

2	Date: Day/Month/Year

3	Name, Position and Address of Recipient
	_____
	_____
	_____
	_____

4	Re: Why you are writing the letter?

5	Dear Mrs O'Connell,

6a	Beginning: 'With reference to your advertisement …'

6b	Middle: Skills … (Refer to the text in question and refer to LCVP/Link Modules if applicable)

6c	End: 'I look forward to hearing from you …'

7	Yours sincerely,

8	Signature

9	Name Typed

10	Enclose: CV

Follow a formal layout with correct grammar. Use paragraphs and check the punctuation.
Make sure there are no spelling mistakes.

Sample letter

70 Ocean View
Church Road
Belmullet
Co. Mayo
Tel: 097-228202

25 March 2016

Mr J. Maher
The Personnel Manager
Kent Communications
23 Halpin Road
Baldoyle
Dublin 13

Re: Application for Store Manager

Dear Mr Maher,

I wish to apply for the position of store manager as advertised in the Irish Independent on Tuesday, 22 March 2016.

I am a 21-year-old business student and am currently participating in a management course. I achieved first-class honours in my business degree at NUIG.

I work on a part-time basis with Castle Computer. I am hardworking and creative, with excellent interpersonal skills.

I would appreciate the opportunity to meet and discuss the matter further. I am available for interview at any time that is convenient for you.

I look forward to hearing from you.

Yours sincerely,

Steven Gallagher

Steven Gallagher

Enclose: Curriculum Vitae

Other letters:

- Inviting a speaker to the classroom
- Organising a visit out
- Thank you letter
- Work experience
- Work shadow
- Researching a career

Application Forms

Most application forms are simple documents that basically just ask for information contained in your CV (personal details, qualifications, skills, etc.). However, some forms are more detailed and require much more thought. You may be asked to explain why you are suitable for the job, which can help you prepare for the interview.

Normally, applications are designed to get standard information about every applicant and they don't allow for flexibility. Sometimes they are poorly designed and don't allow enough space for your answer.

Guidelines for successful form filling

- Read the form carefully and thoroughly.
- Have your CV beside you for reference and to copy from it if you need to.
- Photocopy the form and practise filling it in.
- Begin with the easiest questions.
- Draft the answers to complex questions on a rough piece of paper.
- Fill in all the boxes truthfully. Don't fill in sections marked 'For Office Use Only'.
- If a question does not apply to you, write 'N/A' for 'not applicable'.
- Double-check and proofread the form to make sure there are no spelling or grammatical errors.
- Use a black pen and BLOCK CAPITAL LETTERING.
- Do not use Tipp-Ex or other correction products.
- Make sure your hands are clean before handling the form and keep it in pristine condition.
- Keep a copy of the completed form so that you can look over it again if you are called for interview.

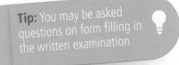

Tip: You may be asked questions on form filling in the written examination

Activity

Practise the above guidelines with a job application form, passport application form and provisional driver's licence form.

Job Offer

Useful words

Words on application forms

Title:	Miss, Ms, Mrs, Mr, Dr
Christian Name:	Your first name, e.g. Mike, Conor, Lil, Shelagh, Marion, Ciara
Surname:	Your family name, e.g. Carew, Walsh, Daly, Hand
Temporary Address:	Where you live at the moment
Home/Permanent Address:	For example, your parents' address
Nationality:	The country you were born in, e.g. Ireland/Irish
Marital Status:	Are you single, married, widowed, etc.?
Next of Kin:	Your closest relative, e.g. wife, husband
Referee:	Name, address and phone number of a person who knows you well and will recommend you for the job. You usually ask your previous employer to be your referee. Remember, you must get permission from referees beforehand and keep them informed about what you are applying for.
Signed:	This is where you put your signature in your own handwriting, e.g. *Gearoid Hourihane*

Most application forms have a box at the end for you to include additional information. This is an opportunity to include anything you did not have a chance to say in the main body of the form.

The computer input type of form is becoming more popular, e.g. CAO applications, so that you can apply online. The same guidelines (e.g. politeness, giving a contact address) apply to using e-mail.

Sample job application form

Using your guidelines for success in form filling, photocopy this page and complete the job application form. Remember, you may also have to complete an application form in the written paper.

APPLICATION FORM
Please complete all sections in your own handwriting.
Use BLOCK CAPITALS.

Surname: **First Name:**

Position Applied For:

Present Address:

Home Address:
(If different to above)

Home Telephone No: **Work Telephone No:**

E-mail Address:

Date of Birth: **Nationality:**

Education

School/Colleges	Years	Examinations Taken	Results

Work Experience (starting with the most recent employment)

Dates	Employer	Position	Reason for Leaving

Interests/Hobbies:

Referees:

I declare that the information contained in this document is correct.

Signature: **Date:**

Curriculum Vitae (CV)

The letters CV stand for the Latin **curriculum vitae**, meaning 'course of life'. A CV is a summary of your education, skills and experience. The purpose of a CV is to help you get an interview for a job. Although there is no one right layout or template, a CV will typically contain the applicant's personal details, qualifications, qualities and skills, work experience, achievements and interests.

In your portfolio, you should not reproduce a CV for a particular job. You should compose a general, all-purpose CV that concentrates on presenting relevant information in a concise and ordered way. For the portfolio, you are encouraged to show evidence of new skills and experience gained during the programme.

Skills and qualities

You may find it difficult to identify and document your skills and qualities.
The following ideas might help you:

- Do a skills audit (see pages 73–4) to measure your practical, technical and interpersonal skills.
- Do a multiple intelligences test (see pages 75–8).
- As you participate in activities during the course of the LCVP, keep note of the skills you have developed and the qualities you have demonstrated.

When presenting your skills and qualities in your CV, you may decide to write a statement **or** to present them as bullet points. Here are some examples.

Statement

'An enthusiastic, self-motivated student who always strives to achieve a very high standard.'

'A good team member with excellent communication skills.'

'A determined, honest and trustworthy school leaver with the ability to motivate others.'

Personal skills and qualities

- Good communication skills
- Flexible and willing to learn
- Good organisational skills
- Very creative

A **personal profile/statement** says what is special about you.

You may decide to continually **update** your personal statement as you take part in LCVP activities. This will help you to write your statement of skills and qualities.

Do not copy the above. Ensure your skills and qualities are related to the content of your CV.

Tip:
2 pages maximum

Guidelines for CV Structure

1. **Personal details**	These may include your name, address, telephone number and date of birth. A student is not required to give details such as nationality, gender or religion on the CV and may prefer not to show date of birth. The CV must be **signed** and **dated**.
2. **Education/ qualifications**	This will include names of schools, years attended, dates of examinations and subjects, including levels and grades. In most cases, the examinations will comprise the Junior Certificate (results) and the Leaving Certificate (to be taken). Don't forget to include Link Modules.
3. **Work experience**	Start with the most recent work placement, giving dates (including year), name of position, employer (both name and address and a summary of responsibilities). Be sure to develop your points and responsibilities.
4. **Achievements**	School related, personal or sporting.
5. **Interests and hobbies**	Examples.
6. **Additional information**	Membership of a club, ability to speak a language.
7. **Referees**	Give name, job title, address and telephone number.
8. **Your signature and the date**	Sign your CV and include an appropriate date, including the year.
9. **Skills and qualities**	A hardworking, self-motivated school leaver with good communication skills, excellent organisational skills and a high level of interpersonal skills.

You may decide to continually update your personal statement as you take part in LCVP activities. This will help you to write your statement of skills and qualities.

Tip: Before you start your portfolio, revise the ten tips for perfecting your portfolio on pages 190–91.

Curriculum Vitae

Personal details
Name
Address
Telephone
E-mail

Educational details
Primary school
Post-primary

Examinations

Junior Certificate 20_ _

Subject	Level	Grade

Tip: For subject level you may use H for Higher and O for Ordinary.

Leaving Certificate 20_ _

Subject	Level	Grade

Tip: Don't forget that Link Modules is a Leaving Certificate subject.

Work experience

Date
Employer
Duties

Tip: Ensure to give name and address.

Date
Employer
Duties

Interests and hobbies

Achievements

Referees

Tip: Don't forget to include two referees and state their position.

Signed   **Date**

All portfolio items must be consistent. See the tips on page 191.

Revise the ten tips for perfecting your portfolio on pages 190–91.

Checklist for success criteria for a curriculum vitae

When you have finished your curriculum vitae, read the list below to make sure you fulfil the LCVP requirements. Be sure to elaborate and articulate learning for each portfolio item. Go to Section 4: Assessment to check general rules for the portfolio and apply the ten tips for perfecting your portfolio items on pages 190–91.

✓ Is your CV word-processed?

✓ Have you used the Times New Roman font throughout?

✓ Have you corrected any spelling or grammar errors?

✓ Does your CV fit onto two A4 pages?

✓ Have you checked the layout and presentation of your CV?

✓ Have you been consistent in the use of capital letters, underlining, punctuation, tabulation, bold and italics?

✓ Does your CV include four items under 'Personal Details'?

✓ Have you stated at least three skills and three qualities in a written statement?

✓ Did you include your educational qualifications?

✓ Are your educational qualifications listed in reverse chronological order, most recent first (i.e. starting with your Junior Certificate results)?

✓ Did you include the full name and address of each school you have attended?

✓ For your Junior Certificate, did you state the year of the examination, subjects, levels and the grades you received?

✓ For your Leaving Certificate, did you state the year of the examination, subjects and levels you are taking?

✓ Did you include Link Modules (not LCVP) as a Leaving Certificate subject?

✓ Under 'Work Experience', have you included the date of the work experience, the employer's name and address and the main duties you carried out?

✓ Have you listed your achievements, hobbies and interests, giving at least two of each?

✓ Did you give the names of two referees?

✓ Did you state the job title of each referee and make sure their names are spelled correctly?

✓ Did you state the name, address and telephone number of the organisation for each referee?

✓ Have you updated your CV if it has been awhile since you first prepared it?

✓ Proofread your CV to make sure it is free of errors and as perfect as possible.

Work in pairs and use this checklist to evaluate your portfolio. Ask for explanations.

Sample Portfolio Item

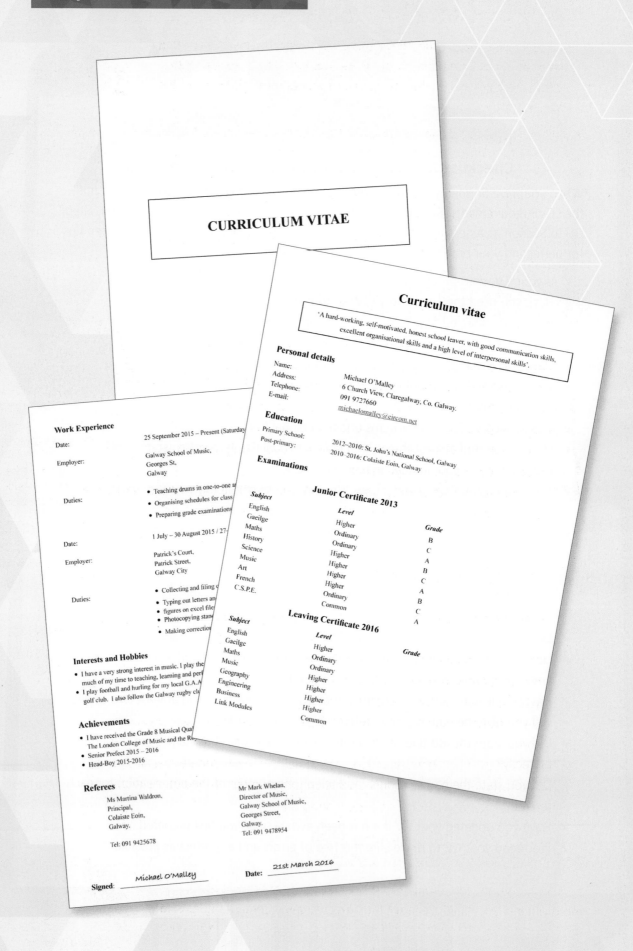

CURRICULUM VITAE

Curriculum vitae

'A hard-working, self-motivated, honest school leaver, with good communication skills, excellent organisational skills and a high level of interpersonal skills'.

Personal details

Name:
Address:
Telephone:
E-mail:

Michael O'Malley
6 Church View, Claregalway, Co. Galway.
091 9727660
michaelomalley@eircom.net

Education

Primary School:
Post-primary:

2012–2010: St. John's National School, Galway
2010–2016: Colaiste Eoin, Galway

Examinations

Junior Certificate 2013

Subject	Level	Grade
English	Higher	B
Gaeilge	Ordinary	C
Maths	Ordinary	A
History	Higher	B
Science	Higher	C
Music	Higher	B
Art	Higher	C
French	Ordinary	A
C.S.P.E.	Common	A

Leaving Certificate 2016

Subject	Level	Grade
English	Higher	
Gaeilge	Ordinary	
Maths	Ordinary	
Music	Higher	
Geography	Higher	
Engineering	Higher	
Business	Higher	
Link Modules	Common	

Work Experience

Date: 25 September 2015 – Present (Saturday

Employer: Galway School of Music,
                 Georges St,
                 Galway

Duties: • Teaching drums in one-to-one a
                 • Organising schedules for class
                 • Preparing grade examinations

Date: 1 July – 30 August 2015 / 27–

Employer: Patrick's Court,
                 Patrick Street,
                 Galway City

Duties: • Collecting and filing
                 • Typing out letters an
                 • figures on excel file
                 • Photocopying stan
                 • Making correction

Interests and Hobbies

• I have a very strong interest in music. I play the
  much of my time to teaching, learning and per
• I play football and hurling for my local G.A.A
  golf club. I also follow the Galway rugby cl

Achievements

• I have received the Grade 8 Musical Qua
  The London College of Music and the R
• Senior Prefect 2015 – 2016
• Head-Boy 2015-2016

Referees

Ms Martina Waldron,   Mr Mark Whelan,
Principal,   Director of Music,
Colaiste Eoin,   Galway School of Music,
Galway.   Georges Street,
                                 Galway.
Tel: 091 9425678   Tel: 091 9478954

Signed: _Michael O'Malley_   Date: _21st March 2016_

Preparing for an Interview

A good cover letter, application form and CV will get you an interview, but you need to do an excellent interview to get the job. Employers are trying to find the most suitable person. You must persuade them that you are the best person for the job.

Remember, your CV and application form show your education, work experience, training accomplishments, skills and qualities. References show your personal qualities and characteristics. However, interviews are the deciding factor. You come face to face with your potential employer and you have to prove yourself.

There are many types of interviews. They vary greatly, but the success of an interview depends on planning.

Pre-interview

- You need to be prepared: research the job and workplace (use the internet to do this).
- Update your CV, making sure to add any new qualifications.
- Practise possible questions and responses. Role-play an interview. Always stress the positive in your answers to questions.
- Organise what to wear and dress neatly and appropriately. Aim for a well-groomed and clean appearance.
- Plan to get to the interview on time. Consider doing a 'dummy run' the day before to check how long it will take you. Allow for delays. Turn up on time.
- Know your strengths and weaknesses. Do a SWOT analysis.

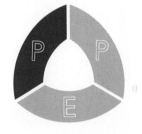

During the interview

- Start with a firm handshake and a smile. This portrays positive body language.
- Establish and maintain eye contact during the interview.
- Communicate positively, clearly and confidently.
- Sit with both feet on the floor and don't slouch.
- Listen attentively and answer truthfully. Expect the unexpected, e.g. awkward or difficult questions.
- Answer all the questions asked. Ask for clarification if you don't understand what is being asked. Have an intelligent question prepared for the end of the interview.
- Thank the interviewer for taking the time to meet you.

Post-interview

If you don't get the job, evaluate the interview and consider what improvements you could make for the next interview. Contact the company and find out how you performed. Try to look at it as a learning experience, which will help you at your next interview.

Evaluating an Interview

The following questions may help you to evaluate your interview:

- What was the best part of the interview?
- What could I have improved on?
- Any additional things I would have liked the employer to know?

Tip: You will leave a lasting impression and improve your chances of success if you follow the above points.

Activity

Take an advertisement for a job from a newspaper. Brainstorm what skills and qualities you have that would suit that position.

Your skills	Your qualities	Which of your skills/qualities are the most relevant to this job?

Which skills are transferable (i.e. which skills can be applied to any job)?

List possible questions that could be asked at an interview.
What questions would be appropriate for the interviewee to ask?

Role Play

Role-play a job interview in pairs without a script. Document the learning.

How Can You Leave a Lasting Impression at an Interview?

1. Be punctual and dress appropriately. Portray a professional image.
2. Speak slowly, clearly and confidently.
3. Know the contents of your CV and that you have researched the company.
4. Portray positive body language with a firm handshake and eye contact.

Learning Board

Key Questions

Answer these questions in your LCVP folder or copybook.

1. Briefly summarise the main points using key words from the unit.
2. Write down something you learned.
3. Write down something you found difficult or challenging.

Devise an Exam Question

Write three exam questions in your LCVP folder or copybook. Start with a quotation, perhaps a specific learning outcome (SLO) or a sentence from this unit.

Presentation

Write a **six-sentence presentation** on recruitment. This can be an individual attempt or work in teams to create a presentation.

Portfolio

Can I use this for my **portfolio**?   Yes ☐   No ☐
The portfolio is worth 60%.

If yes:

CORE – submit all 4

+ Curriculum vitae
+ Enterprise/action plan
+ Career investigation
+ Summary report

OPTIONAL – submit 2 out of 4

+ Diary of work experience
+ Enterprise report
+ Report on 'My Own Place'
+ Recorded interview/presentation

A total of six portfolio items must be submitted.

Tip: Use your portfolio as a revision tool for the written paper

Skills

Now that you have worked through this unit, what are the next steps?
What new skills have you acquired? Describe them.

Tasks

Did you discover any useful websites or YouTube clips?

Learning Board

Cross-curricular

Cross-curricular refers to activities or themes that are relevant to many subjects across the curriculum. For example, health and safety is important in Chemistry, Construction Studies, Engineering, Home Economics and Business.

Answer the following in your LCVP folder or copybook.

1. What Leaving Certificate subjects were useful?
2. How were they useful?
3. Were your vocational subject groupings (VSGs) useful?

Learning Outcomes

Revisit the specific learning outcomes at the beginning of this unit (page 48). Do you understand each SLO?

Key Words

Do you understand the key words on page 48? Write three sentences on each word.

Key Examination Words

Do you understand the key examination words on page 208? For all the main themes, you will need to demonstrate a deep understanding by:

- Describing the term
- Explaining the term
- Demonstrating the term
- Illustrating the term
- Differentiating the term
- Evaluating the term

Tip: This links with Bloom's taxonomy.

Evidence

Tip: Draft a mind map to demonstrate learning in this unit.

You will need to show evidence of your learning. It is your responsibility to keep draft copies of your work. It is a good idea to label and date all activities and handouts in your copy or LCVP folder.

Twenty Sample Questions

The questions on page 70 can first be attempted orally, followed by written answers.

Tip: To improve your examination performance, you need to practise.

Making It Happen: Preparing for Assessment

Assessment ideas based on Preparation for the World of Work
Unit 2 – Job-seeking Skills

Core

➔ **Enterprise/action plan**
  – Plan for a job interview
➔ **Curriculum vitae**

Options

➔ **Recorded interview/presentation**
  – General interview: one or two
    questions on job-seeking skills

 Revise the layout and content of your portfolio items.

➔ **Revise the following:**
  – How are jobs advertised?
  – Write a letter and use a formal layout
  – How to prepare for a job interview
  – How firms recruit, the benefits of using recruitment agencies,
    why employers sometimes have difficulties recruiting and
    how to overcome these difficulties
  – How to apply for a job by telephone
  – Tips for letter writing
  – Guidelines for success in form filling
  – Discuss transferable skills

➔ **Prepare** for questions that show you have participated in an activity.
  Don't forget to use the PEP approach: pre-experience, experience,
  post-experience.

➔ **Cross-curricular learning** – what Leaving Certificate subjects helped you and
  how. Discuss your vocational subject groupings (VSGs) in particular.

➔ **Analyse** your individual contribution and personal performance.

➔ **Evaluation:**
  – How and why do we evaluate?
  – Tips for letter writing
  – Guidelines for success in form filling
  – Discuss transferable skills

Twenty Sample Questions

1. Name **four** different types of application forms you encountered as part of the LCVP.

2. Describe the advice you would give to a student filling in an application form.

3. Indicate how an employer can recruit employees.

4. Write a paragraph outlining why you would prepare for a job interview.

5. Explain **three** rights and **three** responsibilities of an employee.

6. Discuss how you can make a good impression at interviews.

7. List **three** questions you could ask at a job interview and write **three** brief responses.

8. Draft an e-mail applying for a job interview.

9. Comment on future work opportunities.

10. Draft an advertisement for a local company recruiting IT staff.

11. Choose a position for your enterprise activity and list the skills and qualities for this position.

12. Describe how you could demonstrate in an interview that you have good communication skills.

13. Working in teams of four, role-play a job interview.

14. List the different ways jobs can be advertised.

15. Explain the following terms: equal opportunities employer, Safe Pass, CV, referee.

16. Explain why IT skills are important in the workplace.

17. Explain why a broadcasting company would want an employee with good communication skills.

18. Explain why applicants for a job interview are asked to submit references or name a referee in a curriculum vitae.

19. Describe how to leave a lasting impression at an interview in order to improve your chances of success. How would you evaluate your performance?

20. Describe **three** benefits of engaging in further education and training.

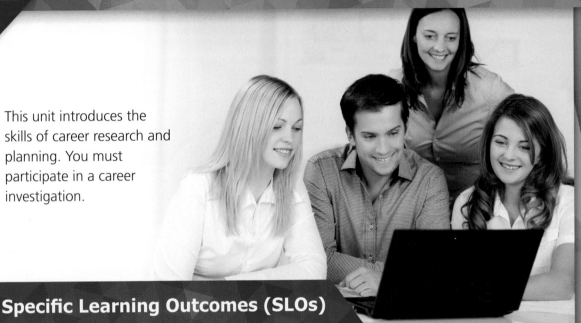

This unit introduces the skills of career research and planning. You must participate in a career investigation.

Specific Learning Outcomes (SLOs)

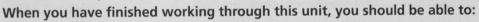

(as listed in the syllabus)

When you have finished working through this unit, you should be able to:

3.1 Identify personal aptitudes and interests

3.2 Investigate a range of careers appropriate to personal aptitude and interests

3.3 Identify and analyse the aptitude and skills required to pursue a specific career

3.4 Describe relevant qualifications and training required for entry to the selected career

3.5 Identify available opportunities to pursue a selected career locally, nationally and, where possible, at international level

3.6 Plan and set up an opportunity to interview and/or work shadow a person in a selected career

3.7 Integrate information from a variety of sources to prepare a final report on a career investigation

3.8 Reflect on and evaluate the experience of undertaking a career investigation

3.9 Link the activities in this unit to learning in relevant Leaving Certificate subjects

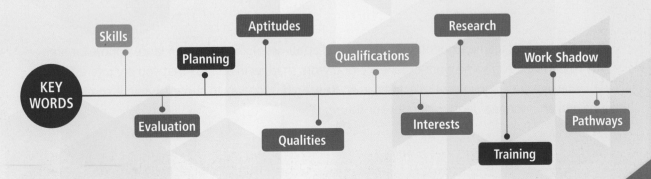

KEY WORDS

Skills · Planning · Aptitudes · Qualifications · Research · Work Shadow · Evaluation · Qualities · Interests · Training · Pathways

A **career investigation** introduces you to the **skills of researching** a career. Ideally, you should look into a career that is related to your interests, your aptitudes (talents and abilities) and to your choice of Leaving Certificate subjects, with particular reference to your vocational subject groupings (VSGs). Before you can do that, you need to become aware of what your abilities, interests and talents are. Only then can you evaluate the vocational options open to you. You will have to change jobs many times throughout your career, so you will also need to know how to find information about career opportunities.

You may research **many careers**, but for the portfolio assessment you show only **one career** that you have researched for your portfolio entry.

To start with, you will need to:

- Assess your skills, qualities, aptitudes, interests and work preferences.
- Find out how information relating to your career choice can be accessed.
- Research the qualifications and training required for that particular job.
- Draw up a contingency plan.
- Interview and/or work shadow someone in your chosen career.

The career investigation is a summary of the information gathered and insights gained while researching your chosen career. The ability to research and plan a career is essential for future employees because you may have to change employment often during your working life. The ability to find information about career opportunities and evaluate your options is a **lifelong skill**. Remember, it is important to engage in a career investigation together with your **guidance counsellor** and other counselling activities in the school.

Choosing a Career

Deciding on your career may be the most important decision that you ever have to make, as it will affect the rest of your life.

You must match your skills, interests and abilities with the options that are available.

Use fifth year as a time to identify your skills and aptitudes. Talk to your guidance counsellor and try to participate in some work experience or a work shadow in an area that you are interested in. Interview a person in your selected career. **Research** is the key to success when it comes to making an informed decision about your future.

Stages of a career investigation

- Compile a personal profile.
- Select your preferred job and conduct research, e.g. career path, skills, qualities, training and qualifications necessary.
- Interview and/or work shadow in your chosen career.
- Submit a career investigation in accordance with the assessment criteria and guidelines.

Skills Audit

You have to become aware of the skills that you have, both as an **individual** (when you are working alone) and/or as part of a **team** (when you work with others). The skills that you demonstrate often depend on the activity that you are engaged in. Participating in a skills audit highlights your highs and also your lows (skills that need to be developed).

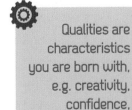

Qualities are characteristics you are born with, e.g. creativity, confidence, honesty.

Personal skills/qualities

I am…

- Honest
- Dependable
- Willing to learn
- Confident
- Determined
- Creative
- Self-motivated
- Aware of my strengths
- Humorous
- Friendly and sociable
- Organised with my time
- Ready to admit mistakes
- Accepting of criticism
- Comfortable expressing my opinion

List your top three personal skills.
What personal skills can you improve on?
Revise skills on pages 12–13.

Tip: Redo this skills test after completing the LCVP. In the written exam, you may be asked to identify personal skills, technical/practical skills and interpersonal group skills.

Technical/practical skills

I am good at…

- Writing reports
- Generating ideas
- Writing letters
- Designing
- Foreign languages
- Speaking on the telephone
- Computer skills
- Working with my hands
- Researching
- Knowledge of materials
- Managing money
- Making things
- Numbers
- Cooking

List your top three technical skills.
What technical skills can you improve on?

Interpersonal/group skills

I can…

Which of these skills and qualities apply to you?

- Work well with others
- Communicate well
- Lead others
- Chair meetings
- Allow others to lead
- Deal with conflict
- Listen to others
- Teach skills to others
- Meet and greet strangers
- Seek the opinion of others
- Ensure others are heard
- Speak in front of a group
- Follow the ideas of others
- Encourage others
- Get on with authority

List your top three interpersonal skills.
What interpersonal skills can you improve on?

Multiple Intelligences: Identifying Your Strengths and Weaknesses

Dr Howard Gardner, a Harvard psychologist, identified at least eight types of intelligences. He was dissatisfied with the narrow range of ability that IQ tests measure. Gardner studied different cultures, brain-damaged adults and autistic children. He wanted to devise a broader concept of intelligence and come up with at least eight systems of learning. Some people excel in one of the eight intelligences at the expense of others, while others have a more balanced profile. Determining your **strengths** and then using them to boost your **weaknesses** can help you to improve your performance in school, further education, your chosen career and in the world of work. Gardner's eight types of intelligences are:

Logical/mathematical	Linguistic/verbal
➜ Good at numbers ➜ Likes to experiment and solve problems ➜ Enjoys working with formulae ➜ Loves the challenge of a complex problem	➜ Good at rhythms and meanings of words ➜ Likes to read, write and listen ➜ Enjoys writing stories ➜ Loves to spell words
Musical	**Spatial/visual**
➜ Good at reproducing melodies ➜ Likes to have music in the background ➜ Enjoys music and rhythmic patterns ➜ Loves mimicking sounds	➜ Good with colours ➜ Likes to think in images and pictures ➜ Enjoys daydreaming ➜ Loves jigsaws and reading maps
Kinaesthetic/body	**Interpersonal**
➜ Good at handling objects ➜ Likes to touch, feel and tap ➜ Enjoys role-play and physical exercise ➜ Loves movement	➜ Good at communicating with others ➜ Likes to work in groups ➜ Enjoys listening and handling conflicts ➜ Loves to respond to the needs of others
Intrapersonal	**Naturalist**
➜ Good at thinking ➜ Likes to work alone ➜ Enjoys reflecting and keeping a journal ➜ Loves meditation	➜ Good at noticing patterns in the environment ➜ Likes to collect items from nature ➜ Loves distinguishing different things in the natural world

Tip: This will help you write a skills and qualities statement for your curriculum vitae.

A Fun Quiz to Spot Your Strongest Intelligence

Read the statements below and make note of the ones that are **true** for you.
Write down your score out of 10.

Linguistic/verbal intelligence

- I enjoy playing with words and doing tongue twisters.
- I enjoy doing crosswords and anagrams and playing word games like Scrabble.
- I sometimes use words that other people don't know.
- I remember the slogans and words from ads more than pictures and images.
- I love reading books.
- I find subjects like English easier than Maths and Accounting.
- I enjoy talking to people about what I have read.
- I enjoy writing essays, diaries, articles and letters.
- I prefer listening to lyrics on my iPod to watching TV.
- I have written something recently that I was proud of or others praised me for.

Logical/mathematical intelligence

$$e = mc^2$$

- New scientific developments fascinate me.
- I love Maths, Accounting and Science.
- I am interested in games like chess and bridge.
- I enjoy identifying patterns and logical sequences in things.
- I love to figure out how things work, e.g. my iPad.
- Adding and subtracting numbers in my head is quite easy for me.
- I believe that almost everything has a rational and logical explanation.
- I get annoyed when other people are not being logical.
- I love to analyse things and put them into categories.
- I like to set up little 'what if' experiments.

Spatial/visual intelligence

- I can read maps quite easily.
- In Maths, I like geometry.
- My dreams are often vivid.
- I have strong opinions about colours I like and dislike.
- I prefer books and magazines that have lots of pictures and images.
- I love putting jigsaw puzzles together.
- I usually manage to find my way around places, even if I don't know them well.
- I love doodling and I like to draw.
- I can visualise descriptions of things easily.
- I enjoy recording what I see by taking pictures or videos on my smartphone.

Kinaesthetic/body intelligence

- I like physical experiences such as bungee jumping.
- I prefer to learn by doing.
- I am involved in sport in my free time.
- I am good at craftwork, Technology and/or Construction Studies.
- I find it hard to sit quietly for long periods.
- I need to touch and feel things in order to learn about them.
- I am very co-ordinated – I am not clumsy.
- I use hand gestures when I am speaking.
- Good ideas often come to me when I am out walking or active in some way.
- I like to spend my free time outdoors when possible.

Musical intelligence

- I often tap rhythmically when studying or working.
- I often find it difficult to stop humming a tune.
- Music plays an important role in my life.
- I am good at remembering melodies after hearing them once or twice.
- Without music, my life would lack something important.
- I am good at singing.
- I love having music playing in the background while I work.
- I know the tunes of lots of songs.
- I play a musical instrument or sing in a choir/band.
- I have a good ear for music and can tell if someone sings off key.

Interpersonal intelligence

- I prefer group sports (e.g. hurling) to solo sports (e.g. running).
- I prefer social games and hobbies (e.g. drama) rather than individual ones.
- I enjoy sharing what I know with others.
- I am often the leader in activities.
- I find that people often ask me for advice.
- Crowds do not make me uncomfortable. I like being surrounded by people.
- I have a few close friends, not just one.
- I get involved in lots of activities connected with my school and the community.
- I am a member of several clubs.
- If I have a problem, I prefer to talk about it instead of solving it by myself.

Intrapersonal intelligence

- I like to keep a diary and reflect on my life.
- I have a hobby or interest that I pursue alone.
- Other people don't always share my opinions.
- I enjoy spending time alone.
- I am aware of my strengths and weaknesses.
- I enjoy meditation.
- I have goals and targets in my life that I think about often.
- I am strong willed and don't mind if other people don't agree with me.
- I would love to run my own business rather than work for someone else.
- I like activities that help me learn more about myself.

Naturalist intelligence

- Environmental pollution bothers me and I am careful not to contribute to it.
- Biology is one of my favourite subjects.
- I recognise different models of car on the road.
- I love walking in the country or by the sea.
- I watch nature programmes on TV.
- When in the countryside, I am very aware of nature and enjoy looking at plants, streams, rocks and flowers.
- I would like to work outside.
- I am interested in the names of plants and trees around me.
- I like gardening.
- When eating or cooking, I think about the ingredients in the food and consider where they have come from and how they are grown.

(Adapted from a quiz in Thomas Armstrong's book *Multiple Intelligences in the Classroom*.)

Results

The key to **multiple intelligences** is that once you have identified your strongest intelligence, you can use your strengths to support your weaknesses. For example, if you are verbally intelligent and have difficulties memorising pictures or images, you could try mentally labelling each part of the picture with a word to make it easier to remember. Or if you are musically intelligent and have difficulty remembering dates, you can try memorising them as lyrics to a familiar tune or rap to aid your memory.

Your strongest intelligence represents the part of your brain that is most active and energetic. When you use that part, you are at your most focused and attentive – you understand and remember things more easily. Use that intelligence to help support your weaker intelligences. Remember, you will need to dedicate more time and energy to whatever intelligence you are weak in if you want to improve. For example, if you are weak linguistically, you can improve this intelligence by reading.

Emotional intelligence (EI) is also important. It is the ability to identify, use and manage emotions in a positive way.

Nobody is strong in all intelligences. If you are weak in one, you will find that you are strong in another. The important thing is to make the most of **your** strengths.

List your top three intelligences. What intelligences can you improve?

Aptitudes

These are your talents and abilities. Your guidance counsellor will usually give you different aptitude tests to help you to identify what you are good at. This type of testing may help you to find suitable careers that match your abilities. There are many different tests that measure areas like verbal reasoning, numerical reasoning, abstract reasoning, etc.

Open Days

Attending open days is another way to research information on your career.

Planning Your Career Investigation

Success is rarely a matter of chance. It is usually the result of careful planning. You must realise the importance of planning. A plan is like a road map showing you where you are now, where you hope to get to and the route you have to take to reach your destination. In planning your career investigation, you must set yourself goals. While planning, you should consider the following. You must be **smart** about your goals or aims when planning.

S	Goals should be **specific**.	Put pen to paper. Writing helps you to focus.
M	Goals should be **measurable**.	I hope to study or work at a particular subject so that I achieve a certain grade.
A	Goals should be **attainable**.	Goals should be achievable. Starting with short-term goals can make long-term goals easier to reach. For example, instead of aiming to go from a D grade to a B, you may decide to go from a D3 to a D1 this term.
R	Goals should be **realistic**.	They should provide neither too great nor too small a challenge.
T	Goals should have **times** attached.	Allow yourself enough time to achieve the goal and to evaluate. Have you achieved what you wanted?

In the Link Modules, you need to:

- Plan for yourself.
- Understand and draft an enterprise/action plan.
- Understand and draft a business plan.

Tip: Use an enterprise/action plan template to plan your career.

Work Shadowing

As part of your career investigation, you must participate in an **out-of-class learning experience**. One such activity may be a work shadow and/or you may decide to participate in a work shadow as part of your work placement. Work shadowing is an excellent opportunity to learn about careers that interest you. Remember, in work shadowing you are **watching** rather than **doing**. It is also an excellent opportunity to improve your communication skills.

⚙ You can submit an enterprise action plan on a career investigation as well as a career investigation itself as long as the plan is not reproduced in the investigation.

Cross-curricular Link with Leaving Certificate Subjects

It is important to relate your Leaving Certificate subjects, especially your vocational subject groupings (**VSGs**), to work/career opportunities.

Careers Associated with Languages

⚙ Revise Unit 4.

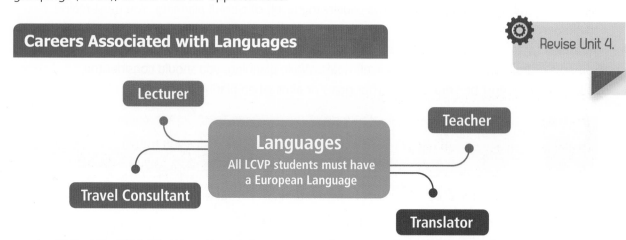

Lecturer

Teacher

Languages
All LCVP students must have
a European Language

Travel Consultant

Translator

Identify other occupations related to European languages.

What careers are linked to your vocational subject grouping (VSG)?

Evaluation is an integral part of your career investigation. Work in pairs and use the following questions to help you with your evaluation of your career.

- What do you have an aptitude for?
- What are you good at?
- Did you do an aptitude test? What did it indicate?
- Does it correspond with what is required for this career?
- What are you interested in?
- What work do you enjoy?
- Was there any aspect of your work experience/summer work/work shadowing/work at home that you liked?
- Is there an individual in a particular career whom you admire, see as a role model or would like to achieve the same success as?
- How do these interests tie in with the career being investigated?

Leaving Certificate subjects

- Outline two subjects you are studying at Leaving Certification level that are most relevant to this career.
- Say how they are relevant to this career.
- Identify what skills or knowledge you have learned in your subjects and how that can be applied in your chosen career.

There are many aspects of evaluation. In the written examination you may be asked to evaluate your career or evaluate participating in your career investigation.

Career Investigation: Interview a Person in Your Selected Career

Here are some possible questions for a career investigation.

Engineering

- What does an engineer do?
- List the different types of engineers.
- What skills does an engineer need to have?
- What qualities do you need?
- What are the career prospects?
- What are the different pathways to pursuing a career in engineering?
- Which pathway did you choose and why?
- Which pathway would you recommend?
- What qualifications and training are needed?
- Are qualifications recognised internationally?
- What salary does an engineer earn?
- Traditionally, would this job have been considered a man's job or a woman's job?
- What are the promotion prospects?
- Do you enjoy your work?
- What's the least interesting part of your work?

Important Guidelines for the Career Investigation

Core item (300–600 words)

1. **Title:** The name of the career being investigated should be displayed prominently.

2. **Description of career:** Three sentences outlining the type of work a person in the chosen career would be doing. All three statements must be different.

3. **Skills and qualities:** List three skills (ability to do the job) and three qualities (type of person, honest, patient, etc.) that are relevant to the chosen career.

4. **Qualifications and training:** You must outline two pathways to your selected job. Make sure both are different. Outline one pathway in detail using the following details:

   - CAO points required
   - Course title
   - College name and location
   - Length of course

   - Details of the course
   - Subjects taught
   - Name of qualification

   What if there is only **one definite route**, e.g. there is only one way to join the gardaí? In this case, describe pathway one and your second pathway can be a contingency plan, e.g. what you will do while you're waiting to train. Will you do a PLC course in security studies?

5. **Interactions:** In developing your research skills, you should refer to interaction with an adult other than teachers in a relevant out-of-class learning experience, e.g. work shadowing, visit to an enterprise, interview with a person in the career area, college open day, careers exhibition or other event organised as part of the school guidance programme. Be specific here. Give the date (including the year) of the interview, the name (Mr, Mrs, etc.) and position of the interviewee and the outcomes of the interview.

6. **Insights gained:** Describe what you learned from the research or activity about your chosen career and about yourself. For example, discuss pay and prospects (locally, nationally and, where possible, at an international level). Be sure to mention the following three points:

   - Leaving Certificate subjects
   - Personal aptitudes
   - Personal interests

7. **Evaluation:**
   - Evaluate the career. Are you still interested in this career? If yes, why are you interested? Be sure to elaborate.
   - Evaluate the skills you developed and the insights you gained from undertaking the career investigation. Be sure to elaborate. Link the benefits to the world of work and further education.

8. **Sources of information:** List any websites, etc. that you used during your career investigation.

Tip: Use a template to record main points or words. Revisit them, elaborate on them and document them in your LCVP folder at a later stage. When you type up your career investigation, make sure to keep a back-up copy on a hard drive.

Career Investigation Template

Tip:
300–600 words

Title: Career investigation of…

Description of career

Skills and qualities

Qualifications and training

Pathway 1

- CAO points required
- Course title
- College name and location
- Length of course
- Details of the course
- Subjects taught
- Name of qualification

Tip: Present the two pathways in a table and it will ensure it's easy to read.

Pathway 2

- CAO points required
- Course title
- College name and location
- Length of course
- Details of the course
- Subjects taught
- Name of qualification

Tip: You must give details for both pathways.

Interactions

Insights gained

Evaluation

Sources of information

 Make sure you are familiar with the required headings. They may be assessed in the written paper.

All portfolio items must be consistent. See the tips on page 191.

Revise the ten tips for perfecting your portfolio on pages 190–91.

Checklist for success criteria for the career investigation

When you have finished your career investigation, read the list below to make sure you fulfil the LCVP requirements. Be sure to elaborate and articulate learning for each portfolio item. Go to Section 4: Assessment to check general rules for the portfolio and apply the ten tips for perfecting your portfolio items on pages 190–91.

- ✓ Did you proofread your career investigation?
- ✓ Have you checked your word count to make sure it is between 300 and 600 words?
- ✓ Did you check for accuracy of presentation and consistency of layout? Check spelling, grammar, capital letters, punctuation, font, headings, tabulation.
- ✓ Have you included a title and named the career you are investigating?
- ✓ Have you described at least three duties involved in the career you investigated, using sentences in each case?
- ✓ Did you name and explain at least three skills required for this career?
- ✓ Did you name and explain at least three qualities needed for this career?
- ✓ Have you described the training needed to become qualified in this career?
- ✓ For each pathway, have you stated the following?
    - – CAO points required
    - – Course title
    - – College name and location
    - – Length of course
    - – Details of the course
    - – Subjects taught
    - – Name of the qualification you will receive at the end of the training period
- ✓ If one of your pathways is not through the CAO system, did you state the entry requirements?
- ✓ Did you carry out research to check your own aptitudes and interests for this career?
- ✓ Did you engage in any out-of-school activity?
- ✓ Did you mention how your Leaving Certificate subjects link to this career?
- ✓ Did you mention how your interests and aptitudes link to this career?
- ✓ Have you evaluated the career? Mention salary, promotion prospects, hours of work and travel prospects.
- ✓ Have you evaluated the process of carrying out the career investigation? State what skills you improved or what new skills you developed.
- ✓ Proofread your career investigation to make sure it is free of errors and as perfect as possible.

Work in pairs and use this checklist to evaluate your portfolio. Ask for explanations.

Interview Structure for the Career Investigation

You may choose to present this portfolio item in the form of an **audio cassette tape** on which you are interviewed for **three to five minutes** about your career investigation.

A possible structure for such an interview, as outlined in **the NCCA Guidelines**, is given below.

1. **Would you like to introduce yourself?** Give your name and candidate number.
2. **You carried out a career investigation as part of your LCVP. What career did you choose to investigate?** Name the career.
3. **Why did you decide to investigate the career of ... ?** Mention your aptitudes, interests and choice of Leaving Certificate subjects.
4. **What exactly does a ... do?** Give a short description of the career.
5. **What skills and qualities would you need for a career in ... ?** 'To be a …, one should have the ability to …' (mention at least three skills, e.g. the ability to operate machinery precisely, the ability to manage people, etc.). 'And one should be the type of person who …' (mention three qualities, e.g. is flexible, has an interest in people, etc.).
6. **What training and qualifications do you need for this career?** Outline two pathways into the career (e.g. two courses you could do, education level or points required for entry, length of study or training, names of qualifications).
7. **What did you do outside the classroom to find out more about this career?** Describe and give the date of work shadowing, interview with a person in the career area or visit to a career-related open day or exhibition.
8. **What do you think you learned from your career investigation?** Evaluate what you learned about the selected career, e.g. 'I found I'm suited to this career because …' Evaluate the experience of doing a career investigation, e.g. 'I learned how to research'; 'I developed communication skills.'

Remember, for the word-processed career investigation, including materials directly downloaded from websites or software packages or copied directly from other sources is not acceptable. However, the inclusion of **specific requirements** downloaded from relevant websites or taken from publications is now permitted because the information is very specific and precise and is difficult to rewrite accurately.

Resources

- A guidance counsellor
- Websites:
  - careersportal
  - cao (courses and links to colleges)
  - vcas (courses in the UK)

Are there opportunities to pursue this career **locally**, **nationally** and at an **international level**?

Mind Map: Outline of a Career Investigation

SKILLS AND QUALITIES
- Skills needed for this job x 3, i.e. abilities
- Qualities needed for this job x 3, i.e. type of person

PATHWAY 1
i. CAO points
ii. Course title
iii. College name and location
iv. Length of course
v. Details of the course: subjects, etc.
vi. Name of qualification

TITLE PAGE
- Title
- Name of career
- Description of career – 3 different sentences

START

END

CAREER INVESTIGATION

PATHWAY 2
- If pathway similar to pathway 1, use same headings
- Otherwise, describe in your own words
- If there is only one definite route, describe a contingency plan

EVALUATION
(A) Career
(B) Experience of undertaking a career investigation

INSIGHTS I GAINED
(A) About the career
(B) About myself

OUT-OF-CLASS LEARNING EXPERIENCE
- Name activity
- Date activity
- What was learned about career?

Sample Portfolio Item

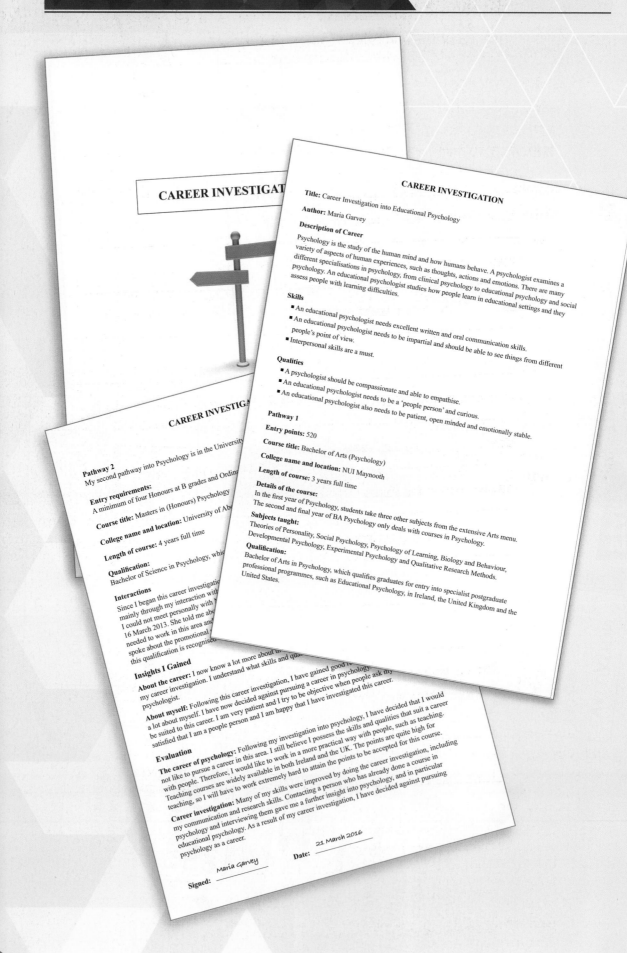

CAREER INVESTIGAT

CAREER INVESTIGATION

Title: Career Investigation into Educational Psychology

Author: Maria Garvey

Description of Career
Psychology is the study of the human mind and how humans behave. A psychologist examines a variety of aspects of human experiences, such as thoughts, actions and emotions. There are many different specialisations in psychology, from clinical psychology to educational psychology and social psychology. An educational psychologist studies how people learn in educational settings and they assess people with learning difficulties.

Skills
- An educational psychologist needs excellent written and oral communication skills.
- An educational psychologist needs to be impartial and should be able to see things from different people's point of view.
- Interpersonal skills are a must.

Qualities
- A psychologist should be compassionate and able to empathise.
- An educational psychologist needs to be a 'people person' and curious.
- An educational psychologist also needs to be patient, open minded and emotionally stable.

Pathway 1

Entry points: 520

Course title: Bachelor of Arts (Psychology)

College name and location: NUI Maynooth

Length of course: 3 years full time

Details of the course:
In the first year of Psychology, students take three other subjects from the extensive Arts menu. The second and final year of BA Psychology only deals with courses in Psychology.

Subjects taught:
Theories of Personality, Social Psychology, Psychology of Learning, Biology and Behaviour, Developmental Psychology, Experimental Psychology and Qualitative Research Methods.

Qualification:
Bachelor of Arts in Psychology, which qualifies graduates for entry into specialist postgraduate professional programmes, such as Educational Psychology, in Ireland, the United Kingdom and the United States.

Pathway 2
My second pathway into Psychology is in the University

Entry requirements:
A minimum of four Honours at B grades and Ordina

Course title: Masters in (Honours) Psychology

College name and location: University of Ab

Length of course: 4 years full time

Qualification:
Bachelor of Science in Psychology, whi

Interactions
Since I began this career investigation
mainly through my interaction with
I could not meet personally with
16 March 2013. She told me ab
needed to work in this area and
spoke about the promotional
this qualification is recognise

Insights I Gained
About the career: I now know a lot more about th
my career investigation. I understand what skills and qua
psychologist.

About myself: Following this career investigation, I have gained good r
a lot about myself. I have now decided against pursuing a career in psychology
be suited to this career. I am very patient and I try to be objective when people ask my
satisfied that I am a people person and I am happy that I have investigated this career.

Evaluation
The career of psychology: Following my investigation into psychology, I have decided that I would
not like to pursue a career in this area. I still believe I possess the skills and qualities that suit a career
with people. Therefore, I would like to work in a more practical way with people, such as teaching.
Teaching courses are widely available in both Ireland and the UK. The points are quite high for
teaching, so I will have to work extremely hard to attain the points to be accepted for this course.

Career investigation: Many of my skills were improved by doing the career investigation, including
my communication and research skills. Contacting a person who has already done a course in
psychology and interviewing them gave me a further insight into psychology, and in particular
educational psychology. As a result of my career investigation, I have decided against pursuing
psychology as a career.

Signed: _Maria Garvey_   Date: _21 March 2016_

Learning Board

Key Questions

Answer these questions in your LCVP folder or copybook.

1. Briefly summarise the main points using key words from the unit.
2. Write down something you learned.
3. Write down something you found difficult or challenging.

Devise an Exam Question

Write three exam questions in your LCVP folder or copybook. Start with a quotation, perhaps a specific learning outcome (SLO) or a sentence from this unit.

Presentation

Write a **six-sentence presentation** on work shadowing.
This can be an individual attempt or work in teams to create a presentation.

Portfolio

Can I use this for my **portfolio**?   Yes ☐   No ☐
The portfolio is worth 60%.

If yes:

CORE – submit all 4

→ Curriculum vitae
→ Enterprise/action plan
→ Career investigation
→ Summary report

OPTIONAL – submit 2 out of 4

→ Diary of work experience
→ Report on 'My Own Place'
→ Enterprise report
→ Recorded interview/presentation

A total of six portfolio items must be submitted.

Skills

Now that you have worked through this unit, what are the next steps?
What new skills have you acquired? Describe them.
Did you participate in teamwork activities? If yes, specify what they were.

Tasks

1. List five questions suitable to ask when interviewing a person in your career.
2. List three careers that you have investigated.
3. Identify skills and qualities associated with the career you investigated.
4. Evaluate your career choice in terms of personal attributes and Leaving Certificate subjects.
5. Did you discover any useful websites/YouTube clips?

Learning Board

Cross-curricular

Cross-curricular refers to activities or themes that are relevant to many subjects across the curriculum. For example, health and safety is important in Chemistry, Construction Studies, Engineering, Home Economics and Business.

Answer the following in your LCVP folder or copybook.

1. What Leaving Certificate subjects were useful?
2. How were they useful?
3. Were your vocational subject groupings (VSGs) useful?

Learning Outcomes

Revisit the specific learning outcomes on page 71.
Do you understand each SLO?

Key Words

Do you understand the key words on page 71? Write three sentences on each word.

Key Examination Words

Do you understand the key examination words on page 208? For all the main themes, you will need to demonstrate a deep understanding by:

- Describing the term
- Explaining the term
- Demonstrating the term
- Illustrating the term
- Differentiating the term
- Evaluating the term

Tip: This links with Bloom's taxonomy.

Evidence

Tip: Draft a mind map to demonstrate learning in this unit.

You will need to show evidence of your learning. It is your responsibility to keep draft copies of your work. It is a good idea to label and date all activities and handouts in your copy or LCVP folder.

Twenty Sample Questions

Tip: To improve your examination performance, you need to practise.

The questions on page 92 can first be attempted orally, followed by written answers.

Making It Happen: Preparing for Assessment

Assessment ideas based on Preparation for the World of Work
Unit 3 – Career Investigation

Portfolio of coursework – 60%

Core

- → **Enterprise/action plan**
  - – Plan for a career investigation
  - – Plan a work shadow placement
- → **Curriculum vitae**

Options

- → **Recorded interview/presentation**
  - – General interview: one or two questions on a career investigation

Revise the layout and content of your portfolio items.

Written paper – 40%

- → **You may be assessed** on the career you investigated, pathways, skills and qualities. Consider the following:
  - – Personal skills
  - – Technical skills
  - – Interpersonal skills
  - – Opportunities to pursue a selected career locally, nationally and, where possible, at an international level
  - – Interviews: pre-interview, during the interview and post-interview
  - – Work shadow: advantages, disadvantages, how to achieve a placement, etc.
  - – Teamwork
  - – How personal targets are reached
- → **Some questions may require** that you demonstrate in your answer that you participated in a career investigation.
- → **Cross-curricular learning** – what Leaving Certificate subjects were useful? How were these subjects useful? In particular, how were your vocational subject groupings (VSGs) useful?
- → **Analyse** your individual contribution and personal performance in this unit.
- → **Evaluation:**
  - – How and why do we evaluate?
  - – How would you evaluate your suitability for the careers you researched?

Twenty Sample Questions

1. Name a career you have investigated.

2. List **three** qualities you have that make this a suitable career for you.

Tip: In the examination, a question will normally have four parts. Revise examination preparation. Be sure to revise Unit 2, as questions can be linked.

3. Identify **two** of your Leaving Certificate subjects that you think are the most relevant for this career. Explain why each subject is relevant.

4. Describe how you went about investigating the career you chose.

5. Identify and analyse **three** aptitudes or skills that are needed for this specific career.

6. Having identified a suitable career, describe **three** steps you now need to take to reach your career goal.

7. Describe **three** methods of evaluating the career investigation activity.

8. Identify **three** sources of information you used to investigate the career. Outline how each source was relevant.

9. Describe **three** changes in Irish employment trends in recent years.

10. What are the career prospects locally, nationally and internationally for the career you investigated?

11. What options are available to you if you become unemployed and you wish to return to work?

12. As part of your investigation, you were involved in an out-of-school activity. What were the benefits of participating in this activity?

13. What advice would you give to a recently qualified person who is finding it difficult to get a job in their chosen career area?

14. Describe ways in which participating in the LCVP may improve your career opportunities.

15. What information would a personal profile contain? Write a brief account of yourself. Make sure to include aptitudes, interests, subject choices and work experience.

16. Comment on the importance of planning your career investigation.

17. Draw up an agenda for a class meeting to organise a career exhibition.

18. List categories of exhibitors you would invite to a career exhibition. Draft a letter inviting a speaker to discuss careers.

19. How would you evaluate a careers exhibition your class organised? Discuss the importance of evaluation.

20. List qualities that employers may look for.

Tip: Skim Section 4: Assessment, in particular the section on revising exam questions (pages 202–205).

In this unit, you are encouraged to plan, organise and engage in a **work placement** (work experience/work shadowing). If possible, the placement should be consistent with your career aspirations. This gives practical experience of the adult working environment as well as helping to develop your skills. Ensure it is a placement over the two years of the LCVP only, usually in year 1 of the LCVP. Transition year work experience is not accepted.

Specific Learning Outcomes (SLOs)

(as listed in the syllabus)

When you have finished working through this unit, you should be able to:

4.1 Specify personal goals in relation to a work placement

4.2 Plan and organise a work placement

4.3 Attend punctually for a specific placement

4.4 Dress appropriately for a specific placement

4.5 Follow a set of procedures in accordance with specific instructions

4.6 Communicate effectively with other workers in a particular placement

4.7 Follow a specific set of instructions relating to health and safety

4.8 Review personal experiences in relation to a work placement

4.9 Analyse reports by adults of personal performance in a workplace

4.10 Reflect on and evaluate a specific work placement in the light of career aspirations

4.11 Describe how what has been learned can be applied to work at home, in school and in the community

4.12 Present a diary/written/verbal report on a specific work placement

4.13 Link the activities in this unit to learning in relevant Leaving Certificate subjects

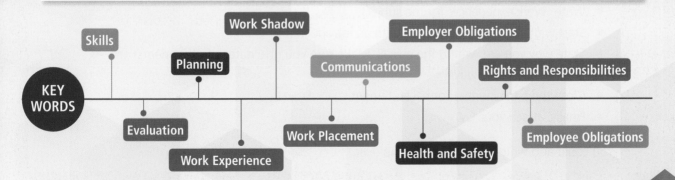

KEY WORDS

Skills · Planning · Work Shadow · Communications · Employer Obligations · Rights and Responsibilities · Evaluation · Work Experience · Work Placement · Health and Safety · Employee Obligations

Work Placement: Work Experience or Work Shadowing

Work placement is a key component of the LCVP. From a learning perspective, work placements are a very powerful activity. You might only engage in a limited amount of work, but you can learn by observing, interacting and communicating with adults in the workplace. It is an ideal opportunity to explore your career aspirations and interests while also learning from debriefing, reflection and evaluation.

Revise Unit 2: Job-seeking Skills.

It is also a chance to try out your **job-seeking skills** from Unit 2 as well as other skills acquired during the LCVP, especially enterprise. The minimum time you should be involved in work-related activities outside the school is **five days**.

You may decide to do a work shadow along with other out-of-school work-related visits, e.g. a two-day shadow or a visit to college open days. If you decide to opt for a work shadow, one of the daily entries may be about preparation for the work shadow or it may be possible to engage in a **five-day work experience**.

You are encouraged to find your own placement. It is important to see the placement as an educational activity and not to expect payment.

A work placement can be seen as giving you a real taste of the world of work. The more prepared you are, the more worthwhile the work placement will be.

As with all LCVP activities, much time is given to the **learning cycle**.
How can you get a suitable work placement?

 PEP

- Prepare a CV.
- Research the company and actual work.
- Talk to a guidance counsellor.
- Write a letter or e-mail or telephone an employer following all you learned in the LCVP.
- Prepare for interview. Try to anticipate questions and prepare draft answers.
- Contacts you have from part-time work might be able to help you get a work placement.

Applying for a Work Placement

When applying for your work placement, you may decide to send an e-mail rather than a letter. Make sure you follow the same formal procedures:

Revise the layout of a letter in Unit 2.

- Have an appropriate e-mail address.
- Write 'Work experience' for the subject.
- Start with an opening, followed with an introduction.
- State why you are writing the e-mail. Make sure you give dates of placements and the number of days.
- Close the e-mail with a formal statement.
- Finally, attach your CV.

You could also write a **letter** to the employer.

Work Experience

This involves gaining experience in a particular work environment by carrying out particular tasks and engaging in duties associated with that type of work.

Advantages

- This type of placement offers an insight into the duties, tasks and responsibilities associated with this type of work.
- This experience can relate directly to your career aspirations.
- During the work experience, you can make contacts for future work, get content for your CV and acquire referees.
- This type of experience will help you develop and improve interpersonal, organisational and communication skills.
- Experiencing a placement can motivate you to work harder.
- You will have the chance to interact with adults other than teachers and parents.
- This experience should be viewed as an opportunity to learn new skills, e.g. teamwork skills, and to acquire new knowledge, e.g. health and safety. You will then be able to apply these skills and knowledge to your home, community and school.

Tip: Use an enterprise/action plan template to plan a work placement.

Work Shadowing

Work shadowing is an alternative to work experience and may also be an option for the career investigation. In work shadowing, your role is to **observe** a working environment and the people in it rather than to engage in tasks. This type of placement allows you to learn about a job by **watching**. Work shadowing does not usually last as long as work experience.

Advantages

- You can expose yourself to a variety of careers.
- This type of placement helps interpersonal and communication skills, as you have to question, which in turn helps develop your interview skills.
- Work shadowing is particularly suitable for careers that don't lend themselves to work experience, e.g. social work.
- During the placement you can make contacts for future work, get content for your CV and acquire referees.
- Since work shadowing placements are shorter than work experience, they can be arranged thought the year and are less disruptive to schools.
- You may be encouraged to sample careers a little bit beyond your reach.
- You can see the world of work and the transition from school to work.
- Experiencing a placement can motivate you to work harder.
- You will have the chance to interact with adults other than teachers and parents.

 Revise rights and responsibilities and legislation (Unit 1) and interview skills (Unit 2).

How can employers ensure a meaningful work experience?

- Provide a detailed job description, including starting times, coffee breaks, lunch time, finishing time, dress code, etc.
- Give students a variety of tasks to perform and allow them to experience all aspects of the job.
- Provide adequate training in terms of induction, health and safety and the use of ICT, including social media.
- Apply all work legislation, including the Young Persons Act and employment equality.
- Allow for interviews and questions to support LCVP.

Preparing for Your Work Placement

Pre-placement

- Set your personal objectives.
- Develop organisation and communication skills.
- Brief employers and parents.
- Prepare a CV.
- Revise letter writing. Practise telephone techniques and e-mail.
- Revise interview techniques.
- Organise transport and inform your principal.
- Get insurance forms and parent consent form.
- Get employer report forms.

Placement

- Find out about the company and its products.
- Make a note of your duties and training.
- Write down your observations.
- Describe the dress code and a typical day.
- Describe your highs and lows.
- Make a note of safety, health and welfare.
- Note any other relevant SLOs.

Post-placement

- What did you learn about the job?
- What skills and qualities are required to do this job?
- Are you suitable?
- How can you improve, overcome problems and master unfamiliar tasks?
- What knowledge and skills can you apply to your home, school and the community?
- Are there career possibilities?
- Did you make contacts for the future?
- What would you do differently?
- Would you recommend the job to others?
- Send a thank you message to the employer, either by letter or e-mail.
- Using the templates on pages 102–106, prepare a Diary of Work Experience.

Employee Characteristics

Employers value certain characteristics in their employees.

An employer may value an employee who is **reliable**. Why? Because it means that they are punctual and turn up on time for work. They will also get the work done properly.

Revise skills and qualities in Unit 2.

Characteristics are similar to qualities. They are part of your personality. You are born with certain characteristics.

Employers also appreciate **hardworking** employees. They will expect employees to do their best and to complete all their work to a high standard. Hardworking employees may also sometimes take on additional work due to staff shortages or extra orders.

Other characteristics that are valued by employers:

- **Team player:** A lot of work requires a team approach, so co-operating and collaborating as a team is a necessity.
- **Trustworthy:** Employees need to be trusted with confidential information and ensuring no property or stock are stolen.
- **Loyalty:** Employees should have the best interests of the employer at heart and always do their best.
- **Initiative:** Employees should be able to deal with work requirements and not have to be given instruction for everything.

Can you name other characteristics and explain why they might be important to an employer?

Communication

Communication is the transfer of information from one person to another. Good communication means information is correctly **given**, **received** and **understood**.

How to Improve Your Communication Skills

- **Practise speaking in public.** This will help you with tone and speed and will help you overcome any feelings of nervousness.
- **Know your subject.** You will come across as more confident and relaxed.
- **Learn to listen carefully.** Listening skills help you to understand and avoid being distracted. Remember, we have two ears and one mouth!
- **Do a communications course.** This will highlight what you need to improve.
- **Join a club**, preferably as an officer (chairperson, secretary, treasurer), so that you will be able to practise communicating.
- **Improve your body language.** Practise in front of a mirror.
- **Practise writing reports and letters.** Make sure you use the appropriate language and that the content and layout are clear.

Sharon Ní Bheoláin is an example of a good communicator.

Importance of Communication Skills

- Good communication means that what you say is accurate, comprehensive (easily understood) and appropriate.
- The ability to communicate well will create a good impression, e.g. with customers.
- Communication skills are a characteristic of entrepreneurs, a desirable quality for employees and a necessary quality for leaders.

Listening as a Communication Skill

DO	DON'T
▪ Show interest	▪ Pass judgement
▪ Encourage	▪ Interrupt
▪ Empathise	▪ Daydream
▪ Ask for clarity if you don't understand	▪ Argue or jump to conclusions

Health and Safety in the Workplace

Don't forget the **Safety, Health and Welfare at Work Act**. During your work placement you must be able to follow instructions relating to the Act. Remember too that both **employers and employees have obligations**. Employees' obligations include the following:

- Follow instructions and be mindful of training.
- Use protective equipment if required.
- Use all equipment in the proper manner and report any dangers or injuries.
- Do not endanger others and look out for safety signs.
- Ask your employer for their Safety Statement.
- Give your insurance details to your employer.
- If you are harassed or bullied, inform your contact person and school.

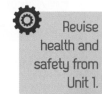

Revise health and safety from Unit 1.

If for some reason you can't attend your work placement, notify the contact person immediately. Don't forget to inform your school too.

Evaluating Your Work Placement

Remember the importance of **evaluation**. How can your work placement be evaluated?

- Your work placement can be evaluated by the quality and content of the work experience diary, especially the evaluation.
- It can be evaluated by getting the employer to complete an evaluation form or by interviewing the employer.
- It can be evaluated by assessing your progress in school after the placement. For example, maybe you are more motivated and are working harder. You can ask your teachers to comment.
- Class discussions on what you learned and how your skills have improved can also be used as a way of evaluating the work placement.

Why is it important to evaluate your work placement?

- To help you make future decisions about your career.
- To review what went well or perhaps what did not go well.
- To identify what areas you need to improve on and how to do things differently.
- To help apply knowledge and skills at home, at school and in the community.
- To reflect on what you learned.

Outline the evaluation prepared as part of the diary of work placement.

1. **Evaluation:** In light of suitability/future studies, Leaving Certificate subjects and career aspirations.
2. **Application:** Being able to apply skills and knowledge to your home, school and community.

Difficulties in Your Work Placement

- Sometimes you may encounter difficulties in your work placement, such as not having enough work to do or even being bored during the placement. Sometimes you may not receive adequate training and may not be able to do the work or follow instructions.
- Some members of staff may exclude you for a variety of reasons. They may not be aware that you are on a work placement if you were not introduced.
- Practical issues may also create challenges for you, such as a dress code, transport or timekeeping.

How Can Your LCVP Work Placement Influence Your Career Choice?

- The actual work you participated in and whether you enjoyed the work.
- The skills required, e.g. communication skills and organisation skills, may have suited your own attributes.
- There may not be any job prospects locally or nationally and you may decide to change your career option.
- Participating in the work placement helped you make an informed decision about your career.

Diary of Work Experience Guidelines for Structure

1. Introductory page	<ul><li>Title.</li><li>Author's name (i.e. your name).</li><li>Dates of work placement, including the year (make sure it is over the two years of the LCVP).</li><li>Name of business or organisation.</li><li>Name of supervisor and their title.</li><li>Position of work placement.</li><li>Duties carried out: Brief summary of duties. You may use bullet points.</li><li>Reasons for selection. These should be consistent with your career aspirations and interests. You might mention things such as choice of Leaving Certificate subjects, aptitudes or interests as reasons for selecting the placement. Alternatively, you might refer to the knowledge, skills and experience you hoped to gain through the placement.</li></ul>
2. Three to five daily entries, which should be clearly dated.	<ul><li>One page per day is recommended. Include the date (including the year), starting time and finishing time on each dated entry.</li><li>Analysis of personal performance. In most cases, the bulk of the daily diary entries will consist of factual descriptions (personalised accounts) of what you observed and experienced during the placement. For example, describe the work, training, skills used, whether you learned anything new, legislation and SLOs (syllabus).</li><li>Evidence of analysis in different situations might include:<ul><li>– How you mastered unfamiliar tasks</li><li>– How you overcame problems or responded to challenges</li><li>– How others viewed your performance</li><li>– How you related to customers and staff</li><li>– What you did well</li><li>– Perhaps a daily evaluation</li></ul></li><li>Make sure you do not repeat daily entries. Use the SLOs to frame your entries.</li></ul>

> The diary of work experience is an outcome of this unit.

Using templates or forms can be a disadvantage if you only answer the questions asked and miss out on other sections. For example, day one may have training while day two may have no training, etc.

3. Evaluation	<ul><li>In reflecting on the placement, consider and record areas such as:<ul><li>– Your suitability to the particular organisation and working environment</li><li>– Career possibilities in the area of work experience</li><li>– Clarify how the experience can help with future studies</li><li>– The relevance of skills gained and contacts made for future career goals</li></ul></li><li>Be sure you discuss Leaving Certificate subjects, study and career aspirations and always elaborate.</li></ul>
4. Application	<ul><li>Include a paragraph describing how you applied (or will apply) the following:<ul><li>– Knowledge (health and safety) gained to your home, school and community</li><li>– Skills (communication skills) gained to your home, school and community</li></ul></li><li>Document both and apply knowledge and skills to all three areas. Always elaborate on your points.</li></ul>
5. Appendix	<ul><li>Up to two appendices may be included, such as:<ul><li>– Employer report</li><li>– Letters, e.g. letter of application, thank you letter</li><li>– Copy of insurance</li><li>– Photo of workplace</li></ul></li><li>Always cross-reference items in an appendix.</li></ul>

It is a good idea to revise skills and qualities in Section 1, along with legislation in Unit 1. This will help you with your work experience diary.

Diary of Work Experience Template

Diary of Work Experience

Name and address of employer:

Tip: 1,000–1,500 words

Dates of work experience:

Title of job:

Job description:

Why I selected this work placement:

All portfolio items must be consistent. See the tips on page 191.

Diary of Work Experience

Day: *One*	**Starting time:**
Date:	**Finishing time:**

Duties performed:

Training:

Instructions:

Interactions with staff/customers:

Observations:

> **Tip:** Headings and templates are a good way to start to structure your portfolio. When completing your portfolio, however, you may not need all these headings.

Problems:

Mastered unfamiliar tasks:

My perception of how others viewed my performance:

> **Tip:** Make sure this reads well. Remember, it's your own view on safety, etc.

Evaluation of today:

Diary of Work Experience

Day: *Two*
Date:

Starting time:
Finishing time:

Duties performed:

Training:

Instructions:

Interactions with staff/customers:

Observations:

Problems:

Mastered unfamiliar tasks:

My perception of how others viewed my performance:

Evaluation of today:

Diary of Work Experience

Day: *Three*   **Starting time:**
Date: **Finishing time:**

Duties performed:

Training:

Instructions:

Interactions with staff/customers:

Observations:

Problems:

Mastered unfamiliar tasks:

My perception of how others viewed my performance:

Evaluation of today:

Diary of Work Experience

Evaluation:

Application:

All portfolio items must be consistent. See the tips on page 191.

Checklist for success criteria for diary of work experience

When you have finished your diary of work experience, read the list below to make sure you fulfil the LCVP requirements. Be sure to elaborate and articulate learning for each portfolio item. Go to Section 4: Assessment to check general rules for the portfolio and apply the ten tips for perfecting your portfolio items on pages 190–91.

- ✓ Is your diary of work experience word-processed?
- ✓ Is the word count between 1,000 and 1,500 words?
- ✓ Does your diary relate to your LCVP work placement?
- ✓ Have you been consistent in your use of punctuation, capitals, font, underlining, etc.?
- ✓ Have you corrected spelling and grammar mistakes?
- ✓ Did you state your name as the author?
- ✓ Have you included the dates of your work experience, including the year?
- ✓ Have you included the title of your job?
- ✓ Have you described the job you carried out on the front page?
- ✓ Have you stated your reasons for choosing this job?
- ✓ Does your reason include career aspirations, skills, Leaving Certificate subjects, interests and aptitudes? Be sure you mention the exact course.
- ✓ Does your document have a clear diary structure?
- ✓ Do you have a minimum of three dated entries?
- ✓ Have you included an analysis of your performance in different situations for each day?
- ✓ Have you evaluated the experience in light of your personal job plans?
- ✓ Have you applied the knowledge gained to home, school and local community situations?
- ✓ Have you applied the skills you learned to home, school and local community situations?
- ✓ Did you submit an appendix with a maximum of two items?
- ✓ Proofread your diary of work experience to make sure it is free of errors and as perfect as possible.

Work in pairs and use this checklist to evaluate your portfolio. Ask for explanations

Mind Map: Outline of a Diary of Work Experience

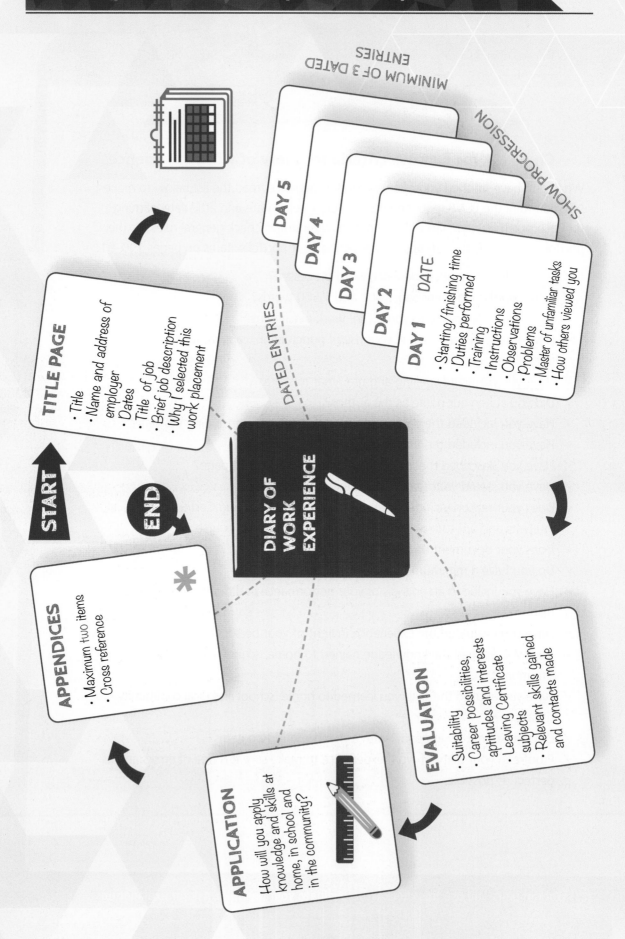

MINIMUM OF 3 DATED ENTRIES

SHOW PROGRESSION

DAY 5

DAY 4

DAY 3

DAY 2

DAY 1 DATE
- Starting/finishing time
- Duties performed
- Training
- Instructions
- Observations
- Problems
- Master of unfamiliar tasks
- How others viewed you

DATED ENTRIES

TITLE PAGE
- Title
- Name and address of employer
- Dates
- Title of job
- Brief job description
- Why I selected this work placement

START

END

DIARY OF WORK EXPERIENCE

APPENDICES
- Maximum two items
- Cross reference

APPLICATION

How will you apply knowledge and skills at home, in school and in the community?

EVALUATION
- Suitability
- Career possibilities, aptitudes and interests
- Leaving Certificate subjects
- Relevant skills gained and contacts made

Sample Portfolio Entry

DIARY OF WORK EXPERIENCE

DIARY OF WORK EXPERIENCE

Name: Mary Carragher

Name and address of employer:
Mr Daniel Hyland,
Principal
_____ rris NS
_____ ris

Day: Monday
Date: 5 October 2015
Starting time: 9
Finishing time:

Duties performed
- Observe the children's daily routine in the Autistic Unit
- Help the children with maths
- Yard duty

Training
I was shown around and introduced to the teachers, SNAs and _____ the children's timetable to me. I was told the rules and _____ was also to _____
policy, whi _____

Instruction
On arrival t _____ Mary. The _____ class work.

Mastered u _____
I began to i _____ but I think I _____ how to copy _____

Daily perfo _____
I thoroughly _____ before. I use _____ ability to dea _____ welcome and _____ take part in _____ attending wit _____

Interactions _____
I had lunch w _____ pursued this _____

Observation _____
I was extreme _____ children felt a _____ talk to me and _____ their maths ac _____

My perceptio _____
I think the sta _____ relieved that _____

Evaluation
I encountered _____ react well with _____ there was no _____ pair of hands a _____

Day: Wednesday
Date: 7 October 2015
Starting time: 9am
Finishing time: 3pm

- Observe and help the children
- Draw posters and assist child to mainstream class
- Yard duty
- Hel _____

_____ to use their program for the

_____ and there was a lot to

Day: Friday
Date: 9 October 2015
Starting time: 9am
Finishing time: 3pm

Duties performed
- Assist the autistic classes on their soci _____
- Assist child to mainstream class

Instructions
As we were going to be walking around _____
watchful eye on the children.
Mastered unfamiliar tasks
I had to laminate the posters we made _____
used one before.

Daily performance
Every Friday the autistic class goes _____
went to the library, the post office, to _____
with them at all times because they _____
ful crossing the road. I was delighte _____
of work experience. We got back a _____
child was particularly delighted an _____
ing it to the SNAs. At the end of t _____
and wind down or chat.

Interactions with staff
As we were out and about I got _____
chat to the other autistic class a _____
that all the staff I encountered _____
children. Being the last day, th _____

Problems I encountered
I thought that the children m _____
behaved well.
My perception of how other _____
I believe the staff realised t _____
acted well with everyone.

Evaluation
I observed that by the end of the week I was more confident, comfortable and at ease about my choice of work experience and I thoroughly benefited from it. The staff said they were delighted to have me there for the week. I was sad that the week was over. I really enjoyed it and I will miss the children. I'm delighted because the week has confirmed to me that I'd like to work with children and/or children with autism.

Overall Evaluation
I was sad that my placement had finished. If I could go there again I would, without a doubt. It was brilliant and I really enjoyed it. I know I have obtained invaluable experience out of this week, more than I ever could have from just reading other people's experiences or course descriptions from the internet. I think I suit this area of work because of my patience, communication and interpersonal skills. I have also developed my adaptability skills this week after being placed in situations that I had never been in before and can definitely be used in the future.

As a result of my work experience I have been researching career possibilities relating to this area of work. The week was more valuable than I ever thought it could have been. I felt great ending each day. Being able to help children is a very rewarding area of work. I made future contacts that I can avail of if I need advice about pursuing a career in this area. I used my creativity skills from Art with the children, as they did their Art class, and my Scientific and Social cooking skills when they were doing their cookery class. I will now research courses on special education training for my CAO application next year.

Application
I have gained a variety of different skills and knowledge as a result of my week's work experience in the Autistic Unit.

Home
I now realise how difficult it is to juggle having a job and working in the home. I have taken more notice of how hard it is for my parents and I will make a much bigger effort to help out at home along with my siblings. I will apply my patience and listening skills. I also learned about health and safety and I will apply this in the home.

School
After my week of work experience I have been truly inspired and realise I have a lot of hard work to do to achieve my goal and study a career I like in third level. I will work very hard to reach my potential. I am much more motivated and focused on school work, as I have had a taste of the type of work I'd like to do in the future. I will now apply my organisation skills and organise my time better. I am delighted to be studying higher level Art and Scientific and Social for my Leaving Certificate, as they can be related to this type of work. I will also apply the knowledge I gained on health and safety in school. I have asked my Link Modules teacher to give a presentation to my class on health and safety.

Community
Following my week's work experience, I will try to fundraise for the Autistic Unit, as they are low on funds and they would like more chances to bring the children outside the classroom and take them on trips. I will apply the organisation skills I developed in my work placement. As I loved the week working with children, I will try to get more experience, and as I have an interest in GAA I will volunteer in the local summer camps this summer. I will also apply the knowledge of health and safety in my role as volunteer.

Employer's Report on LCVP Work Placement

Employer's name and address:

_____

_____

Student's Name:

Attendance date(s):   **No. of days:**

Please tick the following (✓):

	Excellent	Acceptable	Poor	Please comment
Timekeeping				
Relationship with others				
Initiative				
Ability to carry out tasks				
Ability to follow instructions				
Ability to overcome problems				
Attitude towards job				

Any additional information:

_____

_____

_____

_____

Signed: _____

Position: _____ Date: _____

Many thanks for your help with our work placement programme.

Learning Board

Key Questions

Answer these questions in your LCVP folder or copybook.

1. Briefly summarise the main points using key words from the unit.
2. Write down something you learned.
3. Write down something you found difficult or challenging.

Devise an Exam Question

Write three exam questions in your LCVP folder or copybook. Start with a quotation, perhaps a specific learning outcome (SLO) or a sentence from this unit.

Presentation

Write a **six-sentence presentation** on recruitment. This can be an individual attempt or work in teams to create a presentation.

Portfolio

Can I use this for my **portfolio?**   Yes ☐   No ☐
The portfolio is worth 60%.

If yes:

CORE – submit all 4

→ Curriculum vitae
→ Enterprise/action plan
→ Career investigation
→ Summary report

OPTIONAL – submit 2 out of 4

→ Diary of work experience
→ Enterprise report
→ Report on 'My Own Place'
→ Recorded interview/presentation

A total of six portfolio items must be submitted.

Skills

Tip: Use your portfolio as a written revision tool for the written paper.

Now that you have worked through this unit, what are the next steps? What new skills have you acquired? Describe them.

Tasks

1. Draft a note on career possibilities.
2. State three benefits of a work placement.
3. Describe the ways in which participating in the LCVP may improve your career opportunities.
4. Discuss difficulties encountered in your work placement.
5. Did you discover any useful websites/YouTube clips?

Learning Board

Cross-curricular

Cross-curricular refers to activities or themes that are relevant to many subjects across the curriculum. For example, health and safety is important in Chemistry, Construction Studies, Engineering, Home Economics and Business.

Answer the following in your LCVP folder or copybook.

1. What Leaving Certificate subjects were useful?
2. How were they useful?
3. Were your vocational subject groupings (VSGs) useful?

Learning Outcomes

Revisit the specific learning outcomes on page 93.
Do you understand each SLO?

Key Words

Do you understand the key words on page 93? Write three sentences on each word.

Key Examination Words

Do you understand the key examination words on page 208? For all the main themes, you will need to demonstrate a deep understanding by:

- Describing the term
- Explaining the term
- Demonstrating the term
- Illustrating the term
- Differentiating the term
- Evaluating the term

Tip: This links with Bloom's taxonomy.

Evidence

You will need to show evidence of your learning. It is your responsibility to keep draft copies of your work. It is a good idea to label and date all activities and handouts in your copy or LCVP folder.

Tip: Draft a mind map to demonstrate learning in this unit.

Twenty Sample Questions

The questions on page 114 can first be attempted orally, followed by written answers.

Tip: To improve your examination performance, you need to practise.

Making It Happen:
Preparing for Assessment

Assessment ideas based on Preparation for the World of Work
Unit 4 – Work Placement

Portfolio of coursework – 60%

Core

✦ **Enterprise/action plan**
  – Plan a work placement
✦ **Summary report**
  – Work placement (provided you don't submit a work diary in the options)

Options

✦ **Diary of work experience**
✦ **Recorded interview/presentation**
  – General interview: one or two questions on your work placement

Written paper – 40%

✦ **Revise the following topics:**
  – Work placement, how to prepare for it, advantages and disadvantages
  – Health and safety
  – Communications
  – What you learned in your work placement (skills and knowledge) and how it can be applied to work at home, in school and in the community

> Make sure you know the layout and content of your portfolio items.

✦ **Prepare** for questions that demonstrate that you participated in a work placement. Don't forget to use the PEP approach: pre-experience, experience and post-experience. Part of the learning cycle of LCVP is planning, participating and evaluating.

✦ **Cross-curricular learning** – what Leaving Certificate subjects were useful and how? Consider your vocational subject groupings (VSGs) in particular.

✦ **Analyse** your individual contribution and personal performance.

✦ **Evaluation** involves looking at and judging the quality of an activity and asking yourself if you achieved your goals. Consider the following:
  – How and why do we evaluate?
  – Evaluate your work placement.

> **Tip:** When preparing your solutions for these questions, revise Unit 1 and Unit 2.

Twenty Sample Questions

1. Write an e-mail you might send when seeking a suitable work placement.

2. Outline **three** responsibilities you have as an employee to your work placement employer. Describe **three** ways your LCVP work placement has influenced your career choice.

Tip: In the examination, a question will normally have four parts. Revise examination preparation.

3. Outline **two** advantages of work experience.

4. Explain **two** obligations an employer has regarding health and safety at work.

Tip: Revise Unit 1 and Unit 2, as questions can be linked.

5. Outline how you planned for and organised your work placement. Write a brief evaluation of your work placement.

6. List **four** steps you took to secure a suitable placement for your work experience.

7. List and explain **three** personal goals you had in relation to work experience.

8. Describe the steps to take when preparing for a job interview.

9. Why is it important to evaluate your work experience?

10. Outline how you planned for and organised yourself during your work placement/ shadowing.

11. Summarise the evaluation you submitted in your diary of your portfolio.

12. Describe **three** ways in which work experience differs from schoolwork.

13. Identify and explain **four** obligations employees have regarding health and safety at work.

14. Identify and explain the obligations an employer has regarding the health, safety and welfare of their employees.

15. Describe **four** difficulties that a student may experience during their work experience.

16. Write a formal letter to an employer in your area seeking work experience/work shadowing as part of your Link Modules programme.

17. Give **two** criteria you would use to assess how successful your work experience was.

18. Why is feedback important?

19. Communicating with other workers is one area your employer will evaluate you on. Why is communication considered important? If you received an unsatisfactory report in this area, what steps could you take to improve your communication skills?

20. Identify and explain **four** ways you observed health and safety regulations being implemented in the workplace where you did your work experience.

Tip: Skim Section 4: Assessment, in particular the section on revising exam questions (pages 202–205).

The purpose of this unit is to introduce you to the skills of enterprise and entrepreneurship, such as **idea generation**, **risk assessment**, **problem solving**, **teamwork**, **leadership** and **commitment**.

Specific Learning Outcomes (SLOs)

(as listed in the syllabus)
When you have finished working through this unit, you should be able to:

1.1 Describe the qualities and skills of enterprising people

1.2 Recognise examples of personal, community and entrepreneurial enterprise

1.3 Identify personal strengths and weaknesses

1.4 Suggest a course of action appropriate to improving personal enterprise skills

1.5 Work co-operatively with others as part of a team

1.6 Appreciate the value of teamwork in generating ideas, assessing risks, solving problems and completing tasks

1.7 Undertake leadership of a group in an appropriate activity

1.8 Plan and organise a meeting

1.9 Make a presentation to peers and to adults

1.10 Link the activities in this unit to learning in relevant Leaving Certificate subjects

1.11 Evaluate the successes achieved and problems encountered in this unit

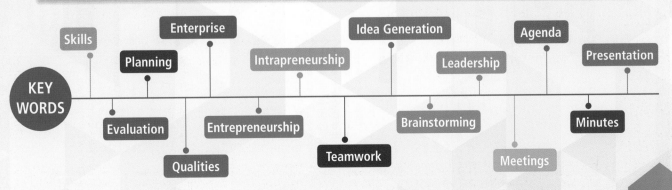

KEY WORDS: Skills, Enterprise, Planning, Intrapreneurship, Idea Generation, Leadership, Agenda, Presentation, Evaluation, Entrepreneurship, Teamwork, Brainstorming, Meetings, Minutes, Qualities

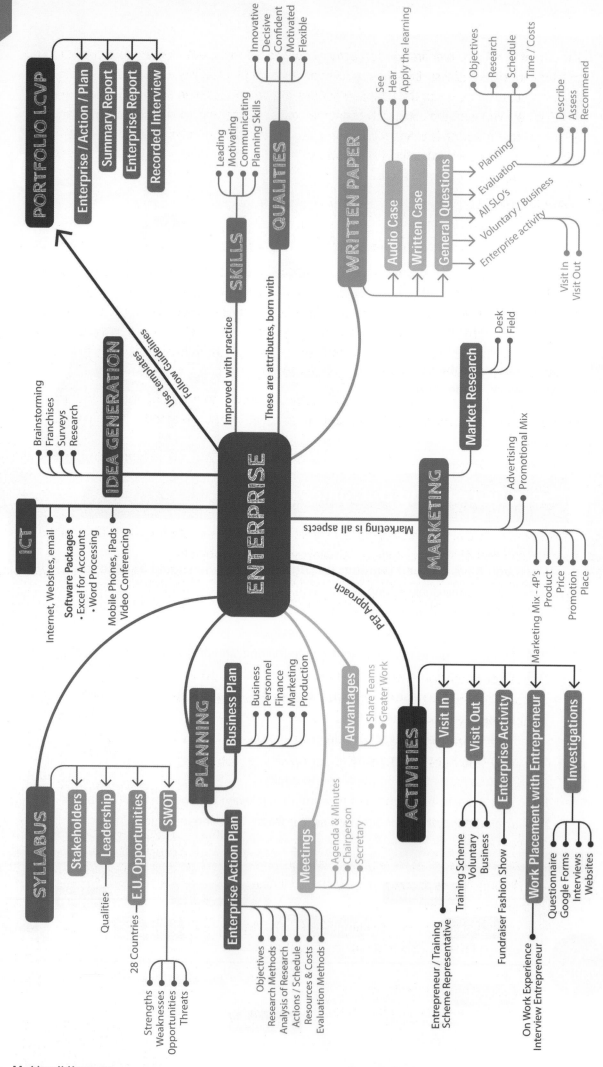

The aim of LCVP is to prepare you for further education, seeking employment and/or planning to start your own business. Enterprise education encourages creativity and problem solving. It creates a culture where you think more readily of setting up your own business in the future. It will also help you with the constantly changing employment situation and our rapidly changing environment. Enterprise is an ideal opportunity to encourage you to be proactive. Furthermore, enterprising people are assets in all areas within the community, whether it is self-employment, being an employer or an active citizen.

Enterprise

Enterprise can be defined as the readiness to engage in bold or difficult undertakings. In order to become more enterprising, you must be aware of the concept of enterprise. Enterprise skills can be observed in local entrepreneurs (people who start their own business). The opportunity to witness at first hand the enterprise skills that they possess can help you to develop an understanding of enterprise in general. Therefore, it is important to establish links with local businesses and community and voluntary organisations.

We often have a narrow misconception of enterprise, associating it with business ventures only. Enterprise affects all aspects of our lives. Enterprise needs to be understood in the broadest possible context:

- Personal enterprise
- Business enterprise
- Community enterprise

Enterprising people are not always entrepreneurs (people who set up a business). They can be found in all walks of life, e.g. students, employees, voluntary workers.

Opportunities to be Enterprising

At school

- You can be enterprising at school by participating in enterprise competitions, e.g. **Student Enterprise Awards, Get Up and Go mini-company competition**.
- You can organise fundraising activities.
- You can set up clubs, e.g. sports clubs or homework clubs.

At home

- You can be enterprising at home by working from home.
- You can be more green by recycling materials, exchanging clothes or recycling clothes by bringing them to charity shops.
- You can rent rooms or set up a home-based industry, e.g. bed and breakfast, home baking and sell at local markets.
- Grow your own vegetables.
- Do some DIY, e.g. painting the house saves on paying a painter.

LCVP is an ideal opportunity to foster young entrepreneurs and to create an entrepreneurial culture in the LCVP classroom.

In your local community

- You can be enterprising by setting up a youth club. This will benefit young people in your locality and possibly avoid local issues such as vandalism.
- You can get involved in local politics.
- You can get involved in charity work by fundraising and improving the needs of particular groups in your local area.
- Neighbourhood watch schemes will ensure that people feel safer, in particular older people or people living alone.

In your personal life

- You can be enterprising by taking courses to develop your talents, e.g. ECDL.
- You can join a sports club to become fit and healthy.
- You can use your skills to help the less fortunate, e.g. doing charity work.

You need to appreciate the different ways in which people are enterprising, either personally, in a business or in the local community.

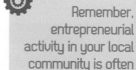

Remember, entrepreneurial activity in your local community is often on a voluntary basis to help improve the community.

In your LCVP folder or copybook, record how you think you are enterprising in different areas of your life.

LCVP is about fostering the attitudes and skills of young people to self-employment, the world of work and further education by developing qualities such as creativity, responsibility, risk-taking, problem-solving, teamwork and experiencing how to run an enterprise activity.

Enterprising People

Enterprising people have a certain set of qualities and develop skills and activities to enhance and complement them.

Enterprising characteristics

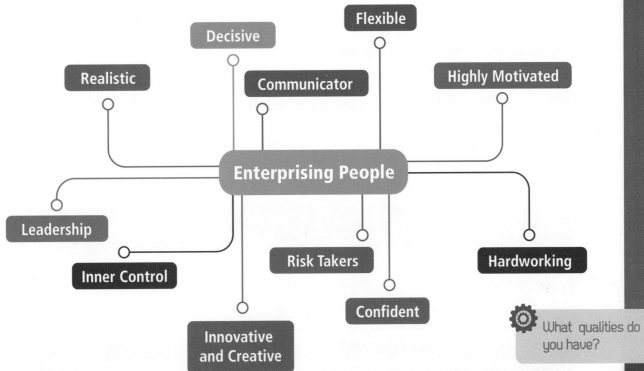

- Flexible
- Decisive
- Communicator
- Realistic
- Highly Motivated
- **Enterprising People**
- Leadership
- Inner Control
- Risk Takers
- Confident
- Hardworking
- Innovative and Creative

What qualities do you have?

Enterprising qualities and skills

Qualities are attributes or characteristics that you are born with. Qualities can be developed.

The following are examples of qualities: confident, ambitious, determined, innovative, risk taker, decisive, hardworking, flexible, ambitious, motivated.

Tip: Revise skills pages 12–13.

Skills are talents that are acquired over time and will improve with training and practice. Skills include the following: planning skills, leading skills, communicating skills, time management skills, motivating skills. You can often justify a quality as a skill and vice versa. Remember to state the difference – if you decide communicating is a skill, do not use this example as a quality in the examination. Remember, there are other skills too, e.g. practical skills such as technology skills.

Enterprising people

Victoria Beckham

Brian O'Driscoll

Louis Walsh

Why are they enterprising?
Can you list Enterprising people in your locality?

As part of your Enterprise Education, you must identify your personal strengths and weaknesses.

My personal SWOT analysis

My strengths: What is going well for me?

In school	At home	In the community

My weaknesses: What is holding me back?

In school	At home	In the community

My opportunities: What is available to me?

In school	At home	In the community

My threats: What aspects are to my disadvantage?

In school	At home	In the community

It is important to know both your strengths and weaknesses. Change your **SWOT** to **SCOT**, where your weaknesses become your challenges. It is also important to know what opportunities are available to you and to become aware of your threats. **Plan** how to overcome these obstacles.

Entrepreneurs

Entrepreneurs are people who have the ability to spot business opportunities, gather the necessary resources, assess risk and take appropriate action to ensure success. They are highly motivated people who calculate risk to achieve their goals. They are essential to our economy. They combine resources such as capital, land and labour to create a successful enterprise. Entrepreneurs need to look before they leap, as some businesses will fail. Some people are enterprising within an organisation. This is called **intrapreneurship**.

 It is a good idea to profile entrepreneurs.

Possible Questions for Profiling an Entrepreneur

Practise questions before you make contact with the entrepreneur. If two or more people will interview the entrepreneur, decide on your roles in advance.

Name: Enterprise:

Why did you set up your business?

What career path did you follow?

Are training and education important?

What are your skills and qualities?

Which skills/qualities are the most important? Why?

What are the benefits of running your own business?

What advice would you give to someone starting his or her own enterprise?

Is location an important factor?

Does the Single European Market impact on your enterprise?

What financial aid or advice did you receive?

What problems did you encounter?

How do you market your product or service?

How do you ensure targets are reached?

What contribution do you make to your local community?

This is a detailed template and will give you extensive information about Entrepreneurs.

Activity

Do you have the characteristics of an entrepreneur? Give yourself a score between 1 and 10, depending on how true you think the following statements are of you. A score of 1 is low and a score of 10 is high. The maximum score is 100.

Characteristic	Explanation	Your score (1 to 10)
1. Innovative and creative	You come up with new ideas or improve on old ones. You find ways of coping. You show creativity.	
2. Risk taker	Entrepreneurs assess and manage risks associated with the venture, both personal and financial. You calculate the possibility of success before any action, i.e. you take measured risks.	
3. Confident	You show belief, optimism and assertiveness.	
4. Decisive	You are able to make speedy decisions and choose a definite course of action.	
5. Inner control	You are able to take control of your own destiny and are extremely determined.	
6. Communicator	You are able to communicate well: information is correctly given, received and understood.	
7. Leadership	You get on well with employees and are able to motivate and encourage staff.	
8. Flexible	You are able to alter plans and adapt as situations change.	
9. Realistic	You know what you can realistically achieve and do not strive for the impossible.	
10. Highly motivated	You need to achieve. You are motivated by money but also personal satisfaction. You enjoy working hard.	

Date: _____   Your score: _____

Try this activity again after participating in the **Link Modules**.

Date: _____   Your score: _____

THINK – PAIR – SHARE

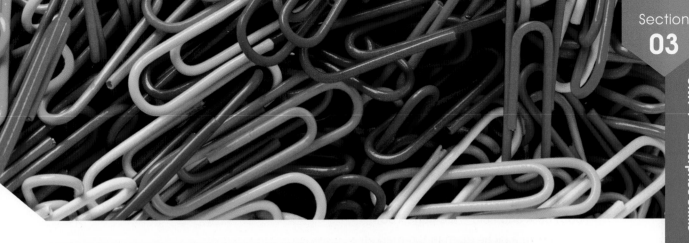

How Does an Entrepreneur Differ from a Manager?

- An entrepreneur comes up with an idea and sets up the business. A manager is responsible for implementing the business and running it on a daily basis.
- An entrepreneur works for themselves. A manager is employed to manage and run the business or organisation.
- The entrepreneur can make lots of money if the business is profitable, whereas the manager usually gets paid a fixed salary. However, the entrepreneur is only being compensated for the risks taken.
- An entrepreneur may not have specific training, whereas a manager does have specific training, usually in one or two specialist areas.

Entrepreneurship in Practice

Idea generation

Every individual has more than 10 billion brain cells, which have unlimited potential. Most people only use 4% to 10% of these cells and the rest are just waiting to be used! It is just a myth that only a small percentage of people are creative. Everyone has an **imagination**, which is the fuel for creative thinking. Sometimes we just need to sharpen our saws.

Have an **ideas page** in your **LCVP folder or copybook** to record unusual or interesting ideas. You may decide to use pictures or photographs. Remember, ideas are central to any business, so it is important to develop innovative and creativity skills.

Start with the paperclip challenge.

How many uses does a paperclip have?

Try this challenge by yourself. Then try it in small groups.

Appoint a group leader, a recorder and a motivator. Think of as many uses as possible and aim for quantity rather than quality. Think of wild ideas, no matter how bizarre. Allow 10 minutes to record the total number of uses.

Write down the total number of uses you thought of on your own.
Write down the total number of uses the group thought of.
Review the group performance in your copybook.

Some strategies to generate ideas:

- Brainstorming with employees, sales staff, etc.
- Mind maps
- Thinking in new ways
- Finding solutions to problems (this could be achieved by research and development)
- Analysing the failures of others
- Finding new uses for products or services (this could be achieved by market research, both desk and field – see page 168)
- Identifying a niche (gap) in the market
- Creating false crises
- Franchising

Idea generation can used to generate ideas for:

- LCVP activities
- Enterprise activities

From idea generation to generating sales

There are a number of stages to follow when developing a product.

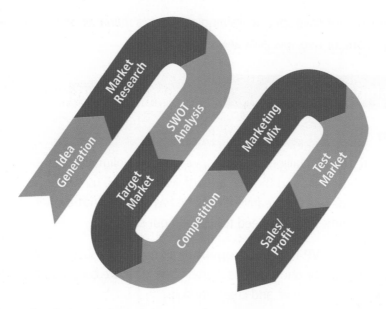

Once you have decided on the product you want to produce or the service you want to provide, you must ensure that it will meet customers' needs. You must have enough **finance** to buy assets and to cover the day-to-day expenses of a business.

Ownership options

There are a number of **ownership options** available to an entrepreneur:

1. A **sole trader** is the name given to a business that is owned and run by one person.
2. A **partnership** describes a business with between two and twenty partners.
3. A **company** describes one of the following:
   - A private limited company
   - A public limited company

The big advantage of a company is **limited liability**, where a company raises capital by issuing shares. If the business goes bankrupt, the owners/shareholders will only lose the money they invested.

A business can be also categorised according to the **number of employees**:

- Small business: 10–50 employees
- Medium business: 50–250 employees
- Large business: More than 250 employees

A micro business has 1–10 employees.

Stakeholders

For a business to succeed, it must deal successfully with all of its **stakeholders**. All stakeholders have an interest in the business.

- **Employers:** The people who hire employees in return for payment. They must abide by all laws, e.g. Safety, Health and Welfare at Work Act 2005. They also have rights and responsibilities.
- **Employees:** The people who work in return for payment. Employees have certain rights and responsibilities.
- **Consumers:** The people who buy goods and services. They want quality and after-sales service.
- **Suppliers:** The people who supply you with raw materials.
- **Investors:** The people or organisations who provide finance, e.g. financial institutions. Finance is provided at a cost, which is called interest.
- **Government:** The government decides on laws and taxes.
- **Trade unions:** The trade unions represent employees and negotiate on their behalf for better wages and conditions.
- **Local community:** The local community is interested in making sure that environmental laws are respected and that infrastructure is provided. They can affect planning applications by lodging objections.
- **Voluntary organisations:** These may look for sponsorship from local businesses.
- **Community enterprises:** Community enterprises encourage local entrepreneurs, e.g. Local Enterprise Offices. They offer advice and finance.
- **Family:** An entrepreneur may have to work long hours, which affects family life.
- **Competitors:** A business has to know its competition, because competition can be a threat to a business.

Teamwork

A team is a group working co-operatively together to achieve a common goal or objective. Teams are widely used in business and local communities and are an integral part of the LCVP. Team-building is a **process** and will not happen overnight.

Review the following:
1. What is your personal experience of the best teamwork situation?
2. What was so special about that team?

Teamwork can enhance the learning in the LCVP classroom. There are many opportunities to experience it during the LCVP, such as planning an activity (e.g. a visit in or a visit out), investigating 'My Own Place' and the LCVP enterprise.

Stages of Team Formation

- **Forming:** When the team comes together and team members are a little unclear.
- **Storming:** Team members are exploring limits. There are a lot of disagreements between members at this stage.
- **Norming:** Team members are beginning to work together and trust develops.
- **Performing:** The team is functioning at its best and has a high level of interdependence.

Advantages and Benefits of Teams

- People working together get more work done.
- Workers take ownership of their work and have responsibilities to others.
- Team members share expertise, skills and responsibilities, which makes difficult work more manageable.
- Working with a team improves relations, makes workers happier and improves motivation.
- Workers with a common interest can work together.
- Teamwork encourages participation and communication, thereby avoiding disputes and improving interpersonal skills.

Challenges and Difficulties of Teams

- Decision making may be delayed because all members need to collaborate.
- Some members may dominate.
- Some members may not be willing to share ideas or the work.

The Ideal Team Member

The ideal team member will be tolerant of other team members' ideas and views. They will be committed to the objectives of the team and ensure deadlines are reached. They will also collaborate and be willing to share all ideas and relevant work.

In order to develop team skills, there are certain things you must do:

- You must listen to each other.
- You should encourage all team members to participate.
- You must record your findings.
- You should seek help if you need it.

Tip: Try to rotate your role in any team activity, e.g. try being the leader, the reporter and then the motivator.

Leadership

Words Associated with Leaders

charismatic, motivational, decisive, consistent, innovative, communicator, optimistic, delegates

Name a leader. Why is he or she a good leader?

A good leader will do the right thing in the right way and make everyone feel good.

They will need to direct and motivate in order to achieve their objectives. They will have many characteristics and will demonstrate their skills and knowledge.

Successful Leaders

A successful leader will do the following:

- They have a knowledge and understanding of all aspects of the work of the business or organisation.
- They are highly motivated and will bring people with them.
- They have excellent communication skills and encourage open communications. They can get their message across in an effective way so that the instructions are acted on. They also listen to avoid being misunderstood.
- They are decisive, can delegate and plan ahead.
- They are innovative and like to try new ideas.

View a YouTube video on leadership.

How Can a Business or Organisation Benefit from Effective Leadership?

- They are more successful and therefore more profitable.
- Employees are content, with good industrial relations, which leads to a reduction in staff turnover and reduces costs.
- Employees are more motivated, which leads to an increase in productivity and hence an increase in profits.
- They will have a good reputation and image, which leads to customer loyalty. In addition, the business or organisation will not have difficulty recruiting.

Characteristics of an Ideal Leader

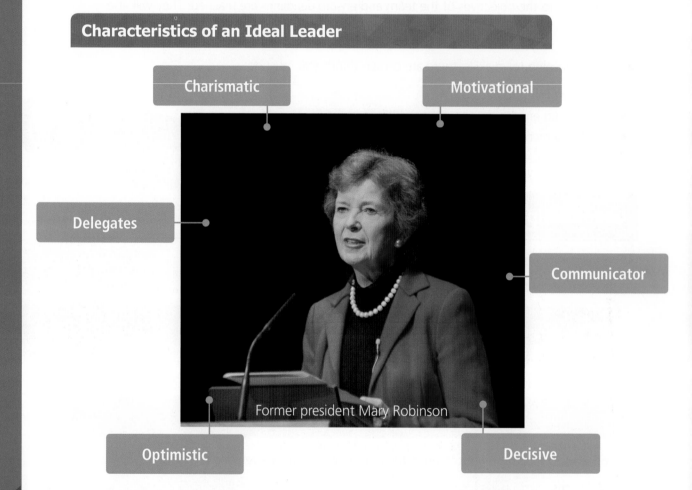

Charismatic

Motivational

Delegates

Communicator

Former president Mary Robinson

Optimistic

Decisive

You must try out a variety of roles in group activities, including that of a leader.

Evaluate Your Role as a Leader

1. Name an activity outside of school in which you acted as a leader.
2. Did you like or dislike the leadership role? Why?
3. Name an LCVP activity in which you acted as a leader.
4. Did you like or dislike the leadership role? Why?

Meetings

A meeting is the coming together of at least two people for a lawful purpose.

Planning and Organising a Meeting

- Send out a notice of the meeting to the people who are invited (usually 10 days before the meeting is due to take place).
- Prepare an agenda (a list of items to be discussed).
- Book a room and ensure it is properly prepared (has the necessary furniture, equipment and documentation).
- Elect a chairperson and a secretary.
- Adhere to the items on the agenda.
- Only allow one person to speak at a time.
- Allow each item to be properly discussed.
- Make sure a written record is being taken. This record is called the minutes.
- Vote properly where and when needed.
- Decide on relevant actions from the meeting.

Important Elements of a Meeting

> ⚙ Topics will vary depending on the type of organisation, e.g. clubs, business enterprises.

Documents

1. **Agenda**

   This is a list of items to be discussed. It should contain the **place**, **date** and **time** of the meeting together with:

   - Minutes of the last meeting
   - Matters arising from the minutes
   - Correspondence
   - Other topics that will vary depending on the meeting
   - AOB (any other business)

2. **Minutes**

   These are a brief written record. They contain the following information:

   - Who attended the meeting
   - The items discussed
   - Any decisions made

People

1. **Chairperson**

   The chairperson has many functions. His or her duties include the following:

   - Convenes the meeting
   - Ensures there is a quorum (minimum number of people)
   - Reads the minutes, which are then proposed and accepted

- Gives speakers time to talk
- Puts motions to a vote. He or she has the casting vote if there is a tie.
- Closes the meeting

2. **Secretary**
   - Calls the meetings
   - Sends out agendas
   - Writes up the minutes

3. **Treasurer**
   - Lodges all the money
   - Keeps accounts
   - Pays the bills
   - Prepares a financial report for the annual general meeting (AGM)

Place

- Put a notice on the door.
- Ensure that there are copies of the agenda for everyone.
- Put place cards, pens and paper on the table.
- Check heating, lighting and ventilation.
- Bring flipcharts or a data projector if needed.
- Bring an attendance sheet.
- Provide refreshments, especially if it is expected to be a long meeting.

Name a meeting you have attended.

Draft an agenda for a meeting.

AGENDA

_____

The meeting will take place at _____ (time) on _____ (date)
in _____ (place).

1. Minutes of previous meeting

2.

3.

4.

5. AOB

Signed: _____   Date: _____

Secretary

> **Tip:** When drafting an agenda, check if it is the inaugural (or first) meeting. There will be no previous minutes.

When drafting the minutes of the meeting, be sure to follow the agenda. State the date, location, who attended the meeting and apologies.

- Commence with approval of agenda
- Review and approval of last meeting's minutes
- Announcements and updates
- Few key topics and actions
- AOB

Learning Board

Key Questions

Answer these questions in your LCVP folder or copybook.

1. Briefly summarise the main points using key words from the unit.
2. Write down something you learned.
3. Write down something you found difficult or challenging.

Devise an Exam Question

Write three exam questions in your LCVP folder or copybook. Start with a quotation, perhaps a specific learning outcome (SLO) or a sentence from this unit.

Presentation

Write a **six-sentence presentation** on teamwork. This can be an individual attempt or work in teams to create a presentation.

Portfolio

Can I use this for my **portfolio**? Yes ☐ No ☐
The portfolio is worth 60%.

If yes:

CORE – submit all 4

→ Curriculum vitae
→ Enterprise/action plan
→ Career investigation
→ Summary report

OPTIONAL – submit 2 out of 4

→ Diary of work experience
→ Enterprise report
→ Report on 'My Own Place'
→ Recorded interview/presentation

A total of six portfolio items must be submitted.

Skills

Now that you have worked through this unit, what are the next steps?
What new skills have you acquired? Describe them.

Tasks

1. Write a brief account of leadership.
2. List the steps to organise a meeting. Draft an appropriate agenda for a voluntary organisation.
3. Discuss idea generation.
4. Did you discover any useful websites?

Learning Board

Cross-curricular

Cross-curricular refers to activities or themes that are relevant to many subjects across the curriculum. For example, health and safety is important in Chemistry, Construction Studies, Engineering, Home Economics and Business.

Answer the following in your LCVP folder or copybook.

1. What Leaving Certificate subjects were useful?
2. How were they useful?
3. Were your vocational subject groupings (VSGs) useful?

Tip: Revisit after completing other units.

Learning Outcomes

Revisit the specific learning outcomes on page 115.
Do you understand each SLO?

Key Words

Do you understand the key words on page 115? Write three sentences on each word.

Key Examination Words

Do you understand the key examination words on page 208? For all the main themes, you will need to demonstrate a deep understanding by:

- Describing the term
- Explaining the term
- Demonstrating the term
- Illustrating the term
- Differentiating the term
- Evaluating the term

Tip: This links with Bloom's taxonomy.

Evidence

You will need to show evidence of your learning. It is your responsibility to keep draft copies of your work. It is a good idea to label and date all activities and handouts in your copy or LCVP folder.

Tip: Draft a mind map to demonstrate learning in this unit.

Twenty Sample Questions

The questions on page 134 can first be attempted orally, followed by written answers.

Tip: To improve your examination performance, you need to practise.

Making It Happen: Preparing for Assessment

Assessment ideas for Enterprise Education
Unit 1 – Enterprise Skills

Core

+ **Enterprise/action plan**
  - Plan a meeting related to an LCVP activity
+ **Summary report**
  - Enterprise activity (provided you do not submit a detailed enterprise report)

Options

+ **Enterprise report:** This unit will help you in writing an enterprise report. Remember, the enterprise report is based on a group enterprise activity (Unit 4)
+ **Recorded interview/presentation**
  - General interview: one or two questions on teamwork, enterprise skills and leadership

Written paper – 40%

+ **Revise the following topics:**
  - Skills and qualities of enterprising people
  - Personal, business and community enterprises
  - Teamwork
  - Idea generation
  - Leadership
  - Plan and organise a meeting
  - Draft an agenda and minutes of a meeting
  - Functions of a chairperson, secretary and treasurer
  - Profile of an entrepreneur
  - Personal SWOT analysis
  - How to improve personal skills and qualities

Revise the layout and content of your portfolio items.

+ **Prepare** for questions that demonstrate you participated in an activity, e.g. a meeting or a team event, a visit by an entrepreneur. Don't forget to use the PEP approach: pre-experience, experience and post-experience. Part of the learning cycle of the LCVP is planning, participating and evaluating.
+ **Cross-curricular learning** – what Leaving Certificate subjects were useful? How were they useful, in particular your vocational subject groupings (VSGs)?
+ **Analyse** your individual contribution and personal performance.
+ **Evaluation** involves looking at and judging the quality of an activity and asking yourself if you achieved your goals. Consider the following:
  - How and why do we evaluate?
  - Evaluate an activity.
  - Evaluate your group performance/teamwork.

Twenty Sample Questions

1. Draft a letter to an entrepreneur inviting him or her to visit the LCVP class.
2. List **five** enterprising skills. Describe **one** in detail.
3. List **five** enterprising qualities. Describe **one** in detail.
4. List non-enterprising skills.
5. Describe how to be a good communicator. Outline ways to improve your communication skills.

Tip: In the examination, a question will normally have four parts. Revise examination preparation.

6. List examples of an LCVP student applying enterprise skills at home, at school and in the local community.
7. As part of the LCVP, you have decided to hold a meeting on LCVP activities. Draft an agenda for the meeting.
8. Describe the necessary steps to ensure a meeting runs smoothly.
9. Your classmates have been asked to evaluate your organisation of a meeting. Describe the different ways that they could evaluate.
10. Describe leadership and discuss what qualities make a good leader.
11. Describe the qualities of an entrepreneur.
12. Describe an entrepreneur you have studied as part of the Link Modules.
13. List **three** personal risks and **three** business risks associated with entrepreneurship.
14. Describe teamwork and the advantages of a team.
15. Discuss the skills required by team members to ensure a highly efficient team.
16. List the difficulties associated with teamwork.
17. Describe the skills and qualities of an effective leader.
18. Draft the minutes of a meeting the LCVP students participated in to plan a visitor to the classroom.
19. Draft suitable headings for a plan to organise a visitor to the LCVP classroom.
20. Discuss how an LCVP student can improve their skills. Evaluate skills developed in the LCVP.

Tip: Skim Section 4: Assessment, in particular the section on revising exam questions (pages 202–205).

The purpose of this unit is to make you aware of what is involved in setting up and running an enterprise. You should be encouraged to meet with entrepreneurs and investigate local business enterprises.

Specific Learning Outcomes (SLOs)

(as listed in the syllabus)

When you have finished working through this unit, you should be able to:

2.1 Identify a range of enterprises in the local community

2.2 Understand how an enterprise starts up and what support/training is available

2.3 Describe the steps required to plan and carry out an investigation of a local enterprise

2.4 Use learning from relevant Leaving Certificate subjects to formulate questions about aspects of a local enterprise

2.5 Organise a visit to a local enterprise and invite appropriate speakers to visit the group in school

2.6 Carry out a SWOT analysis of a business

2.7 Report accurately on a visit by an entrepreneur to the classroom and on a class visit to a local enterprise

2.8 Compare and contrast information gathered on a group visit to a local enterprise

2.9 Describe a local enterprise with particular reference to products, services, markets and workforce

2.10 Understand and describe the different roles of adults working in a business environment

2.11 Describe the impact of the Single European Market on a specific enterprise

2.12 Describe and evaluate the use of information and communication technologies in a business enterprise

2.13 Understand the importance of education and training in the development of a business enterprise

2.14 Link the activities in this unit to learning in relevant Leaving Certificate subjects

2.15 Evaluate the successes achieved and problems encountered in this unit

KEY WORDS: Skills · Planning · Capital · Social Responsibility · Software · Single European Market · Evaluation · Cash Flow · Corporate Responsibility · ICT · Business Plan · SWOT

Local Enterprises in Your Area

Enterprises are important to your local area. You should be aware of the number of businesses in your area and research one in detail.

Benefits of Local Enterprises to the Local Area

Enterprises can benefit the area they locate in.

- They employ local people and have a positive effect on the local economy.
- Other businesses in the area will benefit, e.g. services, banks, transport.
- One business can attract other businesses to the area.
- Enterprises can support local projects, thereby improving the area.
- Enterprises often sponsor local events.
- They may welcome school visits, which is an important LCVP activity.
- Work placements in local enterprises can provide useful experience.
- Local enterprises may agree to school visits.
- The product or service may be produced locally, giving prestige to the area.
- Enterprises often help voluntary and community organisations.
- Local infrastructure benefits from the presence of enterprises.

Evaluating the Success of a Local Enterprise

Success is very important for any business. The following are ways success can be measured.

- **Profitability and sales:** Does the business have high sales and make a profit?
- **Continuity of business:** How long has the business been in existence?
- **Expansion:** Has the business grown? Has the number of staff increased?
- **Awards:** Has the business won any awards?
- **Image:** How is the business regarded by customers? Does it have a good brand image?
- **Low labour turnover:** Do employees stay with the business or do they leave after a short time?
- **Rising share prices:** In the case of a company, has the share price risen?

How a Local Business Can Ensure Targets are Met

- Businesses need to plan carefully and realistically to ensure there is sufficient stock, employees, equipment, etc.
- Businesses could offer incentives, e.g. a bonus or commission, and ask employees to work overtime.
- Businesses need to constantly review and evaluate what is happening and compare planned objectives with actual factors.

Opportunities for You in a Local Enterprise

Investigating a local enterprise will provide you with an ideal opportunity to learn about businesses and to make contacts for future employment. It will also help you to achieve other specific learning outcomes (SLOs).

- Work placements
- Referees for your CV
- Visit in

- Visit out
- Interviews for career investigations
- Contacts for the future

Support and/or Training

When starting a business it is important to be aware of support and training available, such as:

- Local Enterprise Offices
- Údarás na Gaeltachta
- Leader programmes
- Small Firms Association

- Financial institutions
- Enterprise Ireland
- Fáilte Ireland (tourism)
- Bord Iascaigh Mhara (fishing)

Tip: Google what support each organisation offers.

Local Enterprise Investigation

A questionnaire is an ideal way of obtaining information about a company.

- It is a good idea to use the LCVP enterprise/action plan template on page 6.
- Gather as much information as you can about the enterprise before you start the investigation. Does the business have a website?
- You need to be very clear from the start about exactly what information you need to get to complete your investigation. Consider the specific learning outcomes (SLOs).
- Be aware of the assessment criteria – both the written paper and the portfolio. Can you incorporate this investigation into your portfolio?
- Ensure that this activity is relevant to the LCVP and make sure that you achieve the SLOs.
- Plan a visit in or a visit out.

Setting Up an Enterprise: Recipe for Success

There are many difficulties involved in setting up a business: getting enough finance, creating a high-quality product or service that will satisfy potential and existing customers, recruiting and retaining the right staff and choosing the ideal location. You must also try to attract and retain top management, adhere to all legislation and be aware of changes in the economy. To ensure survival, businesses must plan for all of the above. Good planning is the key to success, whether setting up your own enterprise or studying the Link Modules.

Top 10 Factors in the Success of a Business

Considering the factors below will help a business to meet its targets.

Pat McDonagh

1. **Business plan:** A business plan is necessary to apply for loans and grants. It is also useful as a control mechanism. If you don't plan, you might miss opportunities. Use your plan to review and evaluate what is happening and to compare planned objectives with actual results.

2. **Finance**
   - **Capital:** You need money to start a business with in order to purchase equipment, machinery, vans, etc.
   - **Grants:** Research what tax concessions and grants are available.
   - **Other sources:** Finance is also available from bank overdrafts, creditors or from selling shares.
   - **Cash flow:** Cash comes in, cash goes out. This is the money required to run the business.

3. **Product:** There must be a demand for the product. Market research and the marketing mix are very important to identify demand. You also need an adequate promotional mix.

4. **Staffing:** You must have properly trained staff. Consider the following:
   - Recruitment procedures
   - Training
   - Suitable skills and qualities, e.g. willingness to work overtime when under pressure to meet a deadline
   - Incentives, e.g. bonus or commission

5. **Location:** The business needs to be in a good location. Pre-existing premises, for example in a business park, can be a convenient option. Consider the following:

   - Transport services
   - Employees
   - Rail or port if exporting
   - Infrastructure
   - Park may be close to markets
   - Grants – to locate

6. **Managerial experience:** People setting up and running the business must know what they are doing. To run the business effectively, the following are important:
   - **Management skills:** Managers must lead, motivate and communicate.
   - **Management activities:** Managers must also plan, organise and control.

7. **Laws:** Companies must comply with the laws. The following are laws that all businesses must be familiar with:
   - Safety, Health and Welfare at Work Act
   - Employment Equality Act
   - Protection of Young Persons (Employment) Act
   - Sale of Goods and Supply of Services Act
   - Consumer Information Act
   - Tax
   - Maternity leave
   - Data protection

> **Tip:** In LCVP you must know three Acts in detail:
> - Employment equality
> - Health and safety
> - Young persons Act

8. **Economic factors:** The economy plays an important role in the success or failure of a business.
   - The Celtic Tiger caused low interest rates, low taxation and high employment.
   - Recession has now caused the opposite: high interest rates and unemployment.
   - Industrial relations: The relationship between management and employees has a serious effect on business. Avoiding conflict and resolving issues is very important.

9. **Corporate and social responsibility**.

10. **Local environment:** Businesses must obey environmental laws.

> The opposite of these 10 points can cause a business to fail.

Business Plans

Business planning is fundamental to the success of a business. A plan is like a road map and will help you to decide whether you should pursue your business idea or try something else.

You are already familiar with the process of planning and the layout of an **enterprise/action plan**. A business plan is more formal, with a lot of detail on all aspects of the business. The business plan is designed to help you work out how you hope to make the business a success.

Elements of a business plan

A business plan will typically contain the following:

- Description of the business
- Personnel
- Finance
- Marketing
- Production (only if it is manufacturing)
- Other relevant information, e.g. location

Why do the above headings need to be included in a plan?

- **Finance:** You need to know how much money is required so that you can meet day-to-day costs.
- **Personnel:** You need to know the number of employees and the qualifications they need.
- **Marketing:** You need to know your idea will be a success.

A Business Plan

Description of the business

- The business's legal structure: sole trader, partnership or company
- Type of enterprise, e.g. extractive, manufacturing or services
- Product or service: a brief description, patents, etc.

Personnel

- Expertise, experience
- Training
- Qualifications
- Salaries/pay conditions of staff
- Management and their responsibilities
- Departments and organisation structure

Finance

- Capital (money required to start a business)
- Loans (money borrowed from financial institutions)
- Accounts
  - Profit and loss shows net profit or loss
  - Balance sheet shows assets and liabilities
  - Cash flow forecast shows cash in and cash out
- Sources of finance

Marketing

- Market research
- Target market
- Marketing mix: product, price, promotion, place, packaging and personnel
- Advertising
- Competition

Production

- Job production: once-off, e.g. ship building
- Batch production, e.g. baker
- Mass production, e.g. newspapers
- Quality, e.g. Qmark
- Safety (adhering to safety regulations)

Other relevant information

- Leases
- Legal documents
- CVs of key staff
- Patents

When writing a business plan, you might need accounting expertise. Ask Accounting and/or Business students to explain any of the words used above.

Uses of a business plan

1. **Raising finance**
   - A business plan is a requirement for loans and grants.
   - Planning helps you decide how much capital you will need and when it will be needed.

2. **Setting objectives**
   - It is a plan for short-term goals, e.g. to maintain a 5% market share.
   - It is a plan for long-term goals, e.g. expand into the European or world market.

3. **Identifying weaknesses**
   - You need to be aware of your weaknesses and they should become your challenges.
   - You can take corrective action if required.

4. **Controlling/evaluating**
   - A business plan helps you monitor progress by allowing you to compare what actually happens with what was planned.
   - You can test achievements and evaluate performance.
5. **Timing/schedule**
   - Both employees and management know what is to be done and when.

Reasons for preparing a business plan

- A business plan will help you make day-to-day decisions in your business.
- It will help you anticipate business challenges and issues.
- It indicates whether it is worthwhile to start your business or continue your business.
- You can identify how your business is doing by comparing it to the plan (a form of benchmarking).
- Your plan can be a brief for employees.

A plan does not have to be a lengthy document.

Comparing the LCVP enterprise/action plan with a business plan

Enterprise/action plan	Business plan
<ul><li>Objectives</li><li>Research methods</li><li>Analysis of research</li><li>Actions</li><li>Schedule of time</li><li>Resources and costs</li><li>Evaluation methods</li></ul>	<ul><li>Business</li><li>Product or service</li><li>Personnel</li><li>Finance</li><li>Marketing</li><li>Production</li><li>Other relevant information</li></ul>

Important Aspects of Local Enterprises

While conducting your local enterprise investigation, there are certain aspects that you should make sure you pay close attention to. You will need to address these in your investigation:

- ICT
- Single European Market
- Education and training
- SWOT analysis
- Personnel: The role of adults in the workplace

Information and Communications Technology (ICT)

ICT has many uses for enterprises. Find out which of the following technologies your chosen local enterprises use and ask them how important they are to the enterprise. The world has changed significantly in the past 10 years. The rapid development of new technology (free software, free phone calls, wireless connections, tablet computers and smartphones, to name but a few) has changed the way we work and where we work.

1. **The internet:** The internet is a fantastic way of researching information. Businesses can develop their own websites and market products and services worldwide.

2. **E-mail:** E-mail is a cheap way of communicating worldwide. Electronic data interchange allows one computer to connect with another. For example, stock, orders and invoices can be sent from one computer to another, which ensures greater speed.

3. **Software packages:**
   - Word-processing is used for typing letters and reports.
   - Databases are used for filing employee and customer records.
   - The above ensure professional presentation for everything from stationary to PowerPoint presentations.

4. **Mobile phones, portable computers and video conferencing** have dramatically improved communications. It ensures businesses are more efficient and can handle business anywhere. Video conferencing using computer and TV screens is ideal for holding meetings with people all over the world, as it saves time and expenses.

5. **Financial packages:** Spreadsheets and Excel can be used for accounts and payroll. These packages make drawing up budgets an easy task. Online payments have eliminated cheques and are easier to monitor.

Businesses have many uses for computers. The following are some advantages and disadvantages of using ICT.

Advantages of ICT	Disadvantages of ICT
<ul><li>Technology eliminates boundaries worldwide.</li><li>It is possible to work from home.</li><li>Advertising is cheaper on the internet.</li><li>Sending messages is cheap using e-mail.</li><li>Mass production has made technology more affordable and it improves production techniques.</li></ul>	<ul><li>You have to invest a lot of money in technology at first (this is called capital expenditure).</li><li>Staff have to be trained to use the technology.</li><li>Intellectual property rights (copyright programs) are expensive.</li><li>Technology must be constantly updated due to new packages becoming available.</li><li>Fraud can be a problem.</li></ul>

Single European Market

The Single European Market is a group of 28 countries that promote the free movement of goods, services, capital and labour among member countries. Some members also have a common currency, the euro. This has simplified trade and travel in the eurozone.

Impact of the Single European Market

- Irish companies have access to wider European markets.
- Irish companies have more competition. As a result, they have to become more competitive and unfortunately some may close, which may lead to redundancies.
- Many international companies are locating in Ireland to gain access to the European market.
- The introduction of the euro has made it easier to do business in the eurozone (the countries within the EU that have the euro as their currency). Trading outside of the eurozone will expose companies to the risk of currency fluctuations.
- Irish companies have to compete with low-wage Eastern European countries.
- Documentation when trading with EU countries is easier.
- There is greater recognition of qualifications within the EU, which provides more job opportunities.
- Financial institutions are able to open branches in any member state.
- Increased sales, which can lead to economies of scale.
- All contracts over €50,000 for the supply of goods and services to EU governments must be tendered to all EU members. This is known as public procurement.
- There are extra costs involved in the following:
  - Packaging, transport, etc.
  - Interpreters and translators, as modern European language skills are needed to trade with other countries. A modern European language is a requirement of the LCVP.
  - Advertising abroad
  - Adapting products to EU standards and legislation

The European Union

The EU currently has 28 countries, forming a market of nearly 500 million people. Other countries are negotiating entry into the European Union.

The Importance of Education and Training

A wide range of skills, training, education and expertise is required when starting an enterprise. The more education you have, the better. Interestingly, individuals who are more educated are more likely to pursue entrepreneurship. The Global Entrepreneurship Monitor reported that individuals with post-secondary or graduate educations are twice as likely to be involved in an entrepreneurial firm as those with less education. Confidence and role models also have a positive effect on entrepreneurship. Individuals who are confident of their abilities to start and manage a business are four to six times more likely to be involved in entrepreneurship than those who think that they do not have the skills. Therefore, education, knowledge, qualities and training are important for success.

SWOT Analysis

A SWOT/SCOT analysis is an ideal way to assess and investigate a local business.

Internal	Internal
Strengths: These are strong points in the current situation, such as a brand name (e.g. iPad), location, staff, loyal customers, etc. ■ Advantages (the strong points of the business) ■ What is done well	**W**eaknesses/challenges: These are areas that need to be developed, e.g. equipment, management, lack of finance. ■ Disadvantages (areas that the business needs to improve in) ■ What is done badly
External	**External**
Opportunities: These are part of the future possibilities and potential of the business. ■ New markets ■ New trends ■ New products ■ Events	**T**hreats: These are potential dangers. ■ Competition ■ Changes in technology ■ Changes in legislation or government policy ■ Changes in tastes ■ Loss in market share ■ Changes in the economy, e.g. a downturn or recession

Challenges facing business

Businesses face many **uncertainties**. They must be able to **overcome** these challenges.

Possible uncertainties facing a business	How to overcome these challenges
1. Sales level and demand may change	■ Advertise on an ongoing basis ■ Conduct market research constantly ■ Maintain competitive prices ■ Introduce new products or adapt existing range ■ Keep up with changing tastes, technology and laws
2. Difficulties recruiting skilled staff	■ Pay competitive wages ■ Train staff and keep them updated ■ Offer official perks, e.g. company car ■ Establish links with a university, IT, PLC or college ■ Pay college fees (or a proportion of them) for employees who wish to study

3. Availability of adequate raw materials	▪ Produce your own raw materials ▪ Have several suppliers ▪ Develop and source new types of raw materials
4. Profitability	▪ Control your costs and avail of discounts ▪ Ensure an adequate mark-up to allow for profits ▪ Ensure quality
5. Competition	▪ Maintain excellent customer service ▪ Build up customer loyalty
6. Foreign markets	▪ Take advantage of the enlargement of the EU and research new member states (their tastes and laws) as potential customers ▪ Standardise products and services to meet the needs of foreign markets ▪ Trade with countries in the eurozone and with similar tastes

Personnel: The Role of Adults in the Workplace

All stakeholders (who are usually adults) play a role in the workplace. They include the owners, the managers (the leaders), the secretary and employees (professional, skilled, semi-skilled and unskilled), the health and safety officer and the shop steward (union representative). Stakeholders may also be described by function, e.g. manual, clerical, administrative and services.

In a company, the shareholders are the owners. They elect a board of directors, who in turn elect a managing director and CEO. They divide the company into different departments, e.g. production department, purchasing department, sales department and human resource department. All departments have a manager and a supervisor, along with employees.

Invite a speaker to the classroom. However, be sure to select a good speaker. Plan the visit and talk to or e-mail the speaker about the LCVP and send them relevant questions.

Local Enterprise Investigation – Questionnaire

The following shows some possible questions to include in a questionnaire for a local business enterprise. Use it as a guide for creating your own questionnaire and document it in your LCVP folder or copybook. Research the company, make contact and organise an interview. Practise your questions. This is a team activity, so decide on roles in advance (recorder, timekeeper, etc.). You may decide to e-mail the questionnaire to the business.

VISIT OUT　　Name:

Date:　　　　　　　　　　Time:　　　　　　　　Duration:

Details of Visit:

Company

Name:　　　　　　　　　　　　　　　　Website:

Type of Organisation

Sole trader ❑　　Partnership ❑　　Private Company ❑　　Public Company ❑　　Other ❑

Classification

Extractive ❑　　Construction ❑　　Manufacturing ❑　　Tertiary ❑

Comment: _____

_____

Company History

_____

Products/Services

_____

Personnel

Management: _____

Relevant Skills _____ Relevant Activities _____

Qualities of Management _____

Employees

No. of Employees: _____

Male: ❑　　　　Female: ❑

- Who recruits? _____
- How do you recruit? _____
- What type of training do you offer? _____
- What skills and qualities do you look for? _____
- Do you encounter any issues with diversity? _____
- What is the dress code? _____

Are you willing to participate in a work placement for students?　Yes ❑　　No ❑

Marketing

What type of market research do you engage in?

Desk ❑   Field ❑

- Who is your target market? _____
- What percentage of the market share does your company have? _____
- Who is your competition? _____
- Discuss your marketing mix.
    - Product _____
    - Price _____
    - Place _____
    - Promotion _____
- How do you get publicity? _____
- What forms of promotions does your company use?

    Personal Selling ❑   Advertising ❑

    Public Relations ❑   Sales Promotion ❑

Legislation

- Does the company have a Safety Statement? _____
- How do you train personnel with regard to health and safety? _____
- List the main reason for accidents in the workplace. _____
_____
- What is the minimum wage you pay? _____
- Do you promote equality? If so, how? _____

ICT

Do you use ICT? List examples. _____
_____

Does ICT play a major role? How? _____
_____

Have technological changes helped or hindered your business? _____
_____
_____

This is a detailed questionnaire. It will give you extensive knowledge about the business. It will also help you understand key business terms in the LCVP.

Industrial Relations

Are employees members of trade unions? If so, which one(s)? _____

_____

Give typical examples of conflict. _____

_____

How does the company deal with conflicts? _____

_____

Finance

Has the company borrowed money?   Yes ❑   No ❑

If yes, name the financial institution(s) it has borrowed from. _____

Has the company received grants? Comment. _____

List other sources of finance. _____

_____

Production

Type of production: Job ❑   Batch ❑   Mass ❑   Other ❑

Where do you source your raw materials? _____

How do you ensure quality? _____

_____

Support

List any agencies that assisted your company. _____

_____

What type of support did you receive? _____

_____

Europe

What impact does the Single European Market have on your business? _____

_____

Is it important to have knowledge of a European language in your business? _____

_____

Does location matter? Elaborate. _____

_____

Tip: This questionnaire will help you with the written examination.

Learning Board

Key Questions

Answer these questions in your LCVP folder or copybook.
1. Briefly summarise the main points using key words from the unit.
2. Write down something you learned.
3. Write down something you found difficult or challenging.

Devise an Exam Question

Write three exam questions in your LCVP folder or copybook. Start with a quotation, perhaps a specific learning outcome (SLO) or a sentence from this unit.

Presentation

Write a **six-sentence presentation** on SWOT analysis or work in teams to create a presentation. This can be an individual attempt.

Portfolio

Can I use this for my **portfolio**?   Yes ☐   No ☐
The portfolio is worth 60%.

If yes:

CORE – submit all 4
- Curriculum vitae
- Enterprise/action plan
- Career investigation
- Summary report

OPTIONAL – submit 2 out of 4
- Diary of work experience
- Enterprise report
- Report on 'My Own Place'
- Recorded interview/presentation

A total of six portfolio items must be submitted.

Skills

Now that you have worked through this unit, what are the next steps?
What new skills have you acquired? Describe them.

Tasks

1. Identify the impact of the Single European Market.
2. State three benefits of ICT.
3. Are education and training relevant to entrepreneurship?
4. Did you discover any useful websites/YouTube clips?

Learning Board

Cross-curricular

Cross-curricular refers to activities or themes that are relevant to many subjects across the curriculum. For example, health and safety is important in Chemistry, Construction Studies, Engineering, Home Economics and Business.

Answer the following in your LCVP folder or copybook.

1. What Leaving Certificate subjects were useful?
2. How were they useful?
3. Were your vocational subject groupings (VSGs) useful?

Learning Outcomes

Revisit the specific learning outcomes on page 135.
Do you understand each SLO?

Key Words

Do you understand the key words on page 135? Write three sentences on each word.

Key Examination Words

Do you understand the key examination words on page 208? For all the main themes, you will need to demonstrate a deep understanding by:

- Describing the term
- Explaining the term
- Demonstrating the term
- Illustrating the term
- Differentiating the term
- Evaluating the term

Tip: This links with Bloom's taxonomy.

Evidence

You will need to show evidence of your learning. It is your responsibility to keep draft copies of your work. It is a good idea to label and date all activities and handouts in your copy or LCVP folder.

Tip: Draft a mind map to demonstrate learning in this unit.

Twenty Sample Questions

The questions on page 152 can first be attempted orally, followed by written answers.

Tip: To improve your examination performance, you need to practise.

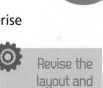

Making It Happen: Preparing for Assessment

Assessment ideas based on Enterprise Education
Unit 2 – Local Business Enterprises

Portfolio of coursework – 60%

Core

- **Enterprise/action plan**
  - Plan an investigation of local enterprises
  - Plan a LCVP visit to a local enterprise
  - Plan a visit to the LCVP classroom by an entrepreneur
- **Summary report**
  - A visit to the LCVP classroom
  - A visit out to an enterprise as part of the Link Modules

Options

- **Enterprise report** – this unit will help you in writing an enterprise report, but remember that the enterprise report is based on a group enterprise activity (Unit 4)
- **Recorded interview/presentation**
  - General interview: one or two questions on this unit

Written paper – 40%

- **Revise the following topics:**
  - Discuss local enterprises and elements of a successful enterprise
  - How to prepare for a visit in
  - How to prepare for a visit out
  - SWOT analysis – success of an enterprise, how to ensure targets, how the enterprise can benefit a locality, how to overcome challenges.
  - Impact of the Single European Market
  - Use of ICT
  - Business plans, layout and reasons for writing a plan
  - The importance of education and training

Revise the layout and content of your portfolio items.

- **Prepare** for questions that demonstrate you participated in an activity, e.g. a visit to an enterprise, a visit by an entrepreneur. Use the PEP approach: pre-experience, experience, post-experience. Part of the learning cycle of the LCVP is planning, participating and evaluating.
- **Cross-curricular learning** – what Leaving Certificate subjects were useful and how were they useful, in particular your vocational subject groupings (VSGs)?
- **Analyse** your individual contribution and personal performance.
- **Evaluation** involves looking at and judging the quality of an activity and asking yourself if you achieved your goals. Consider the following:
  - How and why do we evaluate?
  - Evaluate an activity.
  - Evaluate group performance/teamwork.

Twenty Sample Questions

1. Are education and training relevant to entrepreneurship?

2. Describe an activity you participated in that required teamwork.

Tip: In the examination, a question will normally have four parts. Revise examination preparation.

3. Describe a situation that may give rise to a dispute in a team. If you were the team leader, what action would you take to resolve it?

4. Discuss the uses of a business plan.

5. How can you ensure targets are met in a business?

6. Describe how a business can benefit its local area.

7. Describe uncertainties that a business may face and how to overcome these challenges.

8. Draft a personal SWOT analysis and state the importance of a SWOT analysis.

9. Discuss the impact of the Single European Market.

10. What are the challenges for Ireland as a member of the Single European Market?

11. Discuss the changes in technology over the last 10 years.

12. How has technology changed the way we work?

13. List and explain **five** uses of ICT and what factors a business takes into consideration when deciding where to locate.

14. Outline some of the uncertainties that businesses face.

15. Describe the ways a business can benefit from a local community.

16. Compare and contrast a business plan with an enterprise/action plan.

17. Design a questionnaire to investigate a local business.

18. How can businesses overcome challenges?

19. Discuss the ways to ensure a business will meet its targets in today's economy.

20. Describe how you can evaluate the success of a local enterprise.

Tip: Skim Section 4: Assessment, in particular the section on revising exam questions (pages 202–5).

This unit introduces you to enterprises other than commercial businesses. You are encouraged to find out how these enterprises are organised, how they are funded and how they contribute to local development.

Student Enterprise Awards

Specific Learning Outcomes – (SLOs)

(as listed in the syllabus)

When you have finished working through this unit, you should be able to:

3.1 Identify the voluntary bodies that carry out community work in the locality

3.2 Describe the work carried out by a range of voluntary groups in the locality

3.3 Understand and describe the different roles of adults working in voluntary community organisations

3.4 Organise a visit to a local community enterprise and/or invite an appropriate speaker to visit the group in school

3.5 Use learning from relevant Leaving Certificate subjects to formulate questions about aspects of community enterprise

3.6 Integrate information from a variety of sources to prepare a report, plan or presentation on an aspect of community development

3.7 Link the activities in this unit to learning in relevant Leaving Certificate subjects

3.8 Evaluate the successes achieved and problems encountered in this unit

KEY WORDS

Skills · Planning · Community Organisations · Visit In · Investigation · Fundraiser · Evaluation · Voluntary Organisations · Roles of Adults · Visit Out · Activities

As an LCVP student, you should be aware of the range of voluntary and community activities in your area and the contribution that such activities make to community development. You may decide to profile these community enterprises and voluntary organisations and/or invite a speaker from the organisation to the LCVP classroom. A possible follow-on enterprise activity could be a fundraiser for this organisation. Make sure you know at least one community and one voluntary organisation in detail. Have a general overview of a number of community and voluntary organisations.

Voluntary Organisations

A **voluntary organisation** can be defined as a group of people who have come together on a voluntary basis with the expressed aim of improving the lives of others in the community. These can be divided into local and national organisations. Many voluntary organisations rely on volunteers. Volunteering is the practice of people who work on behalf of others to help them for a particular cause without payment for their time.

National voluntary organisations may have local branches, e.g. Jack and Jill Children's Foundation.

Local voluntary groups and organisations	National voluntary groups
▪ Tidy Towns committees ▪ Youth clubs ▪ Drama clubs ▪ Homework clubs ▪ Neighbourhood Watch	▪ Society of St Vincent De Paul ▪ Trócaire ▪ GAA ▪ Amnesty International ▪ Jack and Jill Children's Foundation ▪ Bubble Gum Club ▪ Focus Ireland

What Do Voluntary Organisations Do?

Voluntary organisations play a significant role in all areas of life and deal with a range of diverse issues. The following table lists a number of voluntary organisations and their main functions.

St Vincent de Paul	Gaelic Athletic Association (GAA)
This is a voluntary organisation whose membership is open to people of all faiths. It aims to help people in need on a person-to-person basis by providing clothing, fuel, food, beds, furniture and holidays.	The GAA was established to revive and nurture traditional indigenous pastimes by the presentation and promotion of hurling, Gaelic football, handball, Irish dancing, music and song. There are over 2,500 clubs in Ireland alone.
Bubble Gum Club	**Jack and Jill Children's Foundation**
The Bubble Gum Club is a charity, registered in Ireland, whose mission is to provide extraordinary outings for extraordinary children, many of whom suffer from life-threatening illness, long-term debilitating illness or are disadvantaged in some other way.	The Jack and Jill Children's Foundation provides direct funding to families of children with brain damage who suffer severe intellectual and physical developmental delay, enabling them to purchase home respite care. These are children who require intensive home nursing care as a result of their condition.

Benefits of Voluntary Organisations

Voluntary organisations benefit the local community in many ways:

- They provide a service that would not otherwise be available.
- They help the less well off in society so that everyone has at least a basic standard of living, e.g. the elderly, the homeless.
- They provide a good example to young people and may encourage them to get involved, which in turn improves their skills.
- The individuals involved benefit through satisfaction. People can also improve skills such as planning, communication and teamwork skills.

Evaluation in Voluntary Organisations

Evaluation is also important for voluntary organisations. Why? Because to evaluate means to look at and judge the quality or value of something. It is important for organisations to take a close look at themselves and what they are doing on a regular basis.

Revise DAR on page 15.

- Evaluation is important because it allows the organisation review what it has achieved.
- The organisation's achievements can be compared with objectives.
- Evaluation provides an opportunity to plan ahead, make improvements and branch out into new areas.
- Evaluation is a chance to check that funds are being properly used.

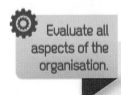

Evaluate all aspects of the organisation.

People Involved in Voluntary Organisations

Revise the visit in and visit out in Section 1.

Most people involved in voluntary organisations work on a voluntary basis. Some people are paid and work on a full-time or part-time basis. People involved in these organisations may have different roles, e.g. counsellors, fundraisers, coaches, managers or administrators. They may have similar positions to a business, i.e. CEO, finance, human resources and secretaries.

A good activity to learn about these organisations is to invite a visitor from the organisation or organise a visit out to one of these organisations as part of the Link Modules.

The templates in this chapter will help you devise questions. You may also be interested in becoming a volunteer. Volunteers would have enterprising skills, personal skills and practical skills.

Community Enterprises

A **community enterprise** is a small commercial enterprise that has been established for the benefit of a local community rather than an individual.

What Do Community Enterprises Do?

Community enterprises promote development in particular communities. The following are some examples outlining the support they offer.

Údarás na Gaeltachta	Leader
Its aim is to preserve and strengthen the Gaeltacht and the Irish language so that strong, self-confident communities can emerge, achieve their full potential and enjoy a high quality of life. This can be achieved by attracting investment to the Gaeltacht regions and offering grants and incentives.	This is an EU initiative for rural development. It enables groups in rural areas to implement their own business plans for the development of their areas. It is co-funded by the Irish government and the EU.

Benefits of Community Enterprises

- Community enterprises help to reduce unemployment.
- They generate income and provide services.
- They restore community pride.
- They improve the local environment.
- They help those who are socially excluded.
- They provide a service that would not otherwise be available.
- They foster greater community spirit, which leads to support when more community projects are undertaken.
- Sometimes they receive grants that are being utilised locally.

Voluntary and Community Organisations vs. Business Enterprises

There are **differences** between voluntary organisations and business enterprises.

> In your LCVP folder or copybook, use the Venn diagram on page 202 to structure an answer for a compare and contrast-type question.

Voluntary organisations	Commercial/business enterprises
■ They are non-profit making ■ Volunteers may receive payment ■ Finance comes from grants, fundraising, lotto ■ They may not have a risk element	■ They trade for a profit ■ Staff receive payment ■ Finance comes from investors and they charge for products or services ■ They have a risk element

The Department of Social Protection has responsibility for community employment and employment services, including advertising a job and finding a job.

Education and training boards have responsibility for the management of training delivery.

Solas focuses on planning, funding and driving the development of a learner-focused integrated further education and training service.

Profile of a Voluntary Organisation Template

Use the following template to profile a voluntary organisation of your choice, e.g. Trócaire.

Name of organisation:	
Services:	**Tip:** Make sure you know at least one voluntary organisation in detail.
Who benefits?	**Website:** **E-mail:**
How is the organisation financed? Do they do any fundraising? If so, how?	**Volunteers/staff and their roles** Qualities and skills Age profile, including minimum age before you can join Paid and unpaid staff
Success	
Day-to-day running of the organisation	
Role in the community	

To source information on voluntary organisations, look up websites, write a letter, e-mail a local representative or invite a speaker from the organisation. A follow-on activity may be a fundraiser for this organisation. If you are writing a summary report on a voluntary organisation, it must be on the activity, e.g. a visitor from a voluntary organisation to the LCVP classroom.

Profile of a Community Enterprise Template

Use the following template to profile a community enterprise of your choice, e.g. Solas.

Name of organisation:	
Services:	**Tip:** Make sure you know at least one community enterprise in detail for the written exam.

Who benefits?	Website: E-mail:
How is the organisation financed? Do they do any fundraising? If so, how?	Volunteers/staff and their roles Qualities and skills Age profile, minimum age if you were to volunteer Paid and unpaid staff

Success

Day-to-day running of the organisation

Role in the community

To source information on community enterprises, look up their websites, write a letter or e-mail to a local representative and/or invite a speaker from this community enterprise to the classroom.

Volunteers

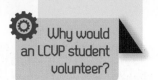

Why would an LCUP student volunteer?

People volunteer for community organisations for a variety of reasons.

- They want to make a difference and contribute to a particular community or society that they or their family may have had experience of, or they may just have an interest. They hope to provide better services for that particular group and improve their life.
- People want to do something positive, especially if they are retired or have free time. They may have recently been made redundant and want to offer their skills and expertise while they wait for employment.
- It can improve personal skills and achieve personal satisfaction. Both society and volunteers benefit. It is also an opportunity to meet people and there may be a social element.
- It can improve your curriculum vitae, as you gain experience as well as referees for future opportunities.

Volunteers also have responsibilities towards the organisation.

- They need to respect the aims and values of the organisation and uphold these values as part of their work. They must also do their work to the highest standard.
- They would also need to maintain confidentiality regarding all aspects of their work and treat members with care, respect and dignity.
- Volunteers need to have and apply all the qualities required from any employer: reliable, hardworking, trustworthy, punctual, dependable, empathy.
- They need to be a team member, work well with other members and share knowledge and skills while constantly up-skilling and training and adhering to these practices in the workplace.

Issues the organisation must consider before recruiting volunteers:

- The organisation must have proper policies, procedures and job descriptions in place. They need to have contracts of employment (see page 28).
- The correct vetting procedures need to be in place.
- They must adhere to legislation, including health and safety, and have adequate insurance.
- They must also provide training if necessary.

Organisations need to evaluate the success of its use of volunteers.

- Retention of staff – there is a problem if volunteers continually leave.
- Design a questionnaire and/or interview volunteers. Discuss their satisfaction levels with regard to the work, the organisation, the management and fellow volunteers.
- Survey the members that avail of the services of the organisation to see if they are content with the service provided.

Businesses can also support voluntary organisations.

- As part of their social and corporate responsibility, businesses can encourage their staff to become volunteers, even during work time.
- They can also give grants or allow the organisations to avail of the business facilities.
- They could also help in fundraising and provide sponsorships.

Why would a business get involved in supporting voluntary organisations?

- It is good for the company's reputation and improves the business's image.
- It improves relationships between the business and the community.
- It generates customer loyalty and so not only benefits the voluntary organisation, but also makes the business more successful.

Learning Board

Key Questions

Answer these questions in your LCVP folder or copybook.
1. Briefly summarise the main points using key words from the unit.
2. Write down something you learned.
3. Write down something you found difficult or challenging.

Devise an Exam Question

Write three exam questions in your LCVP folder or copybook. Start with a quotation, perhaps a specific learning outcome (SLO) or a sentence from this unit.

Presentation

Write a **six-sentence presentation** on a voluntary organisation. This can be an individual attempt or work in teams to create a presentation.

Portfolio

Can I use this for my **portfolio**?   Yes ☐   No ☐
The portfolio is worth 60%.

If yes:

CORE – submit all 4
+ Curriculum vitae
+ Enterprise/action plan
+ Career investigation
+ Summary report

OPTIONAL – submit 2 out of 4
+ Diary of work experience
+ Enterprise report
+ Report on 'My Own Place'
+ Recorded interview/presentation

A total of six portfolio items must be submitted.

Skills

Now that you have worked through this unit, what are the next steps?
What new skills have you acquired? Describe them.

Tasks

1. Write an account on a visitor from a voluntary organisation.
2. List ideas on how to source information on voluntary organisations and community enterprises.
3. How does the work of voluntary organisations contribute to local developments in a community?
4. Describe how you would organise a visitor from a community enterprise.
5. Did you discover any useful websites for voluntary or community organisations?

Learning Board

Cross-curricular

Cross-curricular refers to activities or themes that are relevant to many subjects across the curriculum. For example, health and safety is important in Chemistry, Construction Studies, Engineering, Home Economics and Business.

Answer the following in your LCVP folder or copybook.

1. What Leaving Certificate subjects were useful?
2. How were they useful?
3. Were your vocational subject groupings (VSGs) useful?

Learning Outcomes

Revisit the specific learning outcomes on page 153.
Do you understand each SLO?

Key Words

Do you understand the key words on page 153? Write three sentences on each word.

Key Examination Words

Do you understand the key examination words on page 208? For all the main themes, you will need to demonstrate a deep understanding by:

- Describing the term
- Explaining the term
- Demonstrating the term
- Illustrating the term
- Differentiating the term
- Evaluating the term

Tip: This links with Bloom's taxonomy.

Evidence

You will need to show evidence of your learning. It is your responsibility to keep draft copies of your work. It is a good idea to label and date all activities and handouts in your copy or LCVP folder.

Tip: Draft a mind map to demonstrate learning in this unit.

Twenty Sample Questions

The questions on page 164 can first be attempted orally, followed by written answers.

Tip: To improve your examination performance, you need to practise.

Making It Happen:
Preparing for Assessment

Assessment ideas based on Enterprise Education
Unit 3 – Local Voluntary Organisations and Community Enterprises

Portfolio of coursework: 60%

Core

→ **Enterprise/action plan**

- Plan a LCVP visit to a voluntary organisation or community enterprise
- Plan a LCVP visit in from a representative of a voluntary organisation

Summary report

→ **An LCVP visit** to a voluntary organisation or community enterprise

→ **Visit in** to the Link Modules class from a representative of a voluntary organisation or community enterprise

Written paper: 40%

→ The **ideas** below ensure that you are prepared for all types of questions. Always link the LCVP activities to each unit.

- Be aware of at least one voluntary organisation in detail and have a general overview of a number of voluntary organisations.

> Revise the layout and content of your portfolio items.

- Be aware of at least one community enterprise in detail and have a general overview of a number of community enterprises.

- Compare voluntary organisations with business organisations.

→ **Prepare** for questions that demonstrate you participated in an activity, e.g. visit in, visit out. Don't forget to use the PEP approach: pre-experience, experience, post-experience. Part of the learning cycle of the LCVP is planning, participating and evaluating.

→ **Cross-curricular learning** – what Leaving Certificate subjects were useful and how were they useful, in particular your vocational subject groupings (VSGs)?

→ **Analyse** your individual contribution and personal performance.

→ **Evaluation** involves looking at and judging the quality of an activity and asking yourself if you achieved your goals. Consider the following:

- How and why do we evaluate?

- Evaluate voluntary organisation investigations, visit in/visit out.

- Evaluate group performance/teamwork.

Twenty Sample Questions

1. Compare a voluntary organisation with a community enterprise.

2. Compare a voluntary organisation with a business enterprise.

Tip: In the examination, a question will normally have four parts. Revise examination preparation.

3. What steps should be taken to ensure that the visit in by a volunteer is organised properly and run efficiently?

4. Why it is important to evaluate a visit in by a volunteer?

5. Outline the issues that arise for voluntary organisations.

6. Distinguish between profit-making and non-profit-making organisations.

7. Describe **three** methods that could be used to evaluate the visit out. Give a reason for choosing each method.

8. Your class has decided to organise a visit by a speaker from a local community organisation. List **four** objectives your class might have for this visit.

9. Describe **four** ways the local community benefits from this organisation.

10. Name **three** Leaving Certificate subjects (other than Link Modules) that you are studying and indicate how each was useful in the organisation or planning of a visit out to a community enterprise. How has this activity helped you in each subject?

11. Describe how you could plan a voluntary organisation investigation.

12. Write an e-mail inviting a representative from a voluntary organisation to your Link Modules classroom.

13. Write a letter thanking the speaker from a community organisation who visited the classroom.

14. What are the current challenges facing voluntary organisations?

15. How can local businesses help voluntary organisations?

16. Why do local businesses support voluntary organisations?

17. List **five** questions you would like to ask a volunteer who you have invited into the LCVP classroom.

18. Draft a SWOT analysis of a voluntary organisation you studied as part of the LCVP.

19. List different fundraisers in order to raise finance for a voluntary organisation.

20. Draft an agenda of a meeting of the local GAA club in your area.

Tip: Skim Section 4: Assessment, in particular the section on revising exam questions (pages 202–205).

Link Module 2:
Enterprise Education

UNIT 4:
An Enterprise Activity

This unit provides you with the opportunity to put the skills you have gained in the previous units of the Link Modules into practice. You will **plan, set up and run your own enterprise activities**. Examples are a community survey, a charity fundraiser, publishing a newsletter or local tourist guide, organising a school event or setting up a mini-company to sell a product or provide a service.

Specific Learning Outcomes (SLOs)

(as listed in the syllabus)
When you have finished working through this unit, you should be able to:

4.1 Work co-operatively with others to generate a range of ideas

4.2 Prepare a plan for the selected enterprise activity

4.3 Identify available resources to support an enterprise activity

4.4 Integrate information from a variety of sources, including relevant Leaving Certificate subjects

4.5 Assess personal and group skills and identify possible training needs

4.6 Identify and recruit consultants willing to advise on a selected enterprise activity

4.7 Understand the practical importance of market research and the marketing mix

4.8 Be aware of the concepts of publicity and promotion

4.9 Actively participate in group work in a variety of roles – owner, worker, team leader

4.10 Take responsibility to ensure that targets are reached

4.11 Participate in a review of group performance

4.12 Review personal performance in an enterprise activity

4.13 Prepare and present a written or verbal report on an enterprise report

4.14 Link the activities in this unit to learning in relevant Leaving Certificate subjects

4.15 Evaluate the successes achieved and problems encountered in this unit

KEY WORDS

Skills
Idea Generation
Marketing Mix
Observation
Planning
Questionnaire
Promotion Mix
Evaluation
Brainstorming
Advertising
Questionnaires
Qualities
Market Research

Setting Up an Enterprise

As part of this module, you are encouraged to set up your own enterprise projects as vehicles of learning. You must plan, set up and run your enterprise activities. Examples of possible enterprise activities include organising a fundraiser for your school or local charity; publishing a newsletter, yearbook or musical programme; organising an event, e.g. a careers night or fashion show; producing a local directory; or perhaps setting up a mini-company to sell a product or provide a service. Running an enterprise helps you to get used to making decisions and taking responsibility to ensure targets are reached. Planning will also help you to ensure goals are achieved. You will have to spend extra time on the activity to ensure that it is successful. Continue to use control procedures throughout the project to compare your actual results with planned results to ensure you are on target.

Idea Generation

Firstly, you must generate an idea for your business. You have already studied idea generation in Unit 1 of Link Module 2 (see pages 123–4). Brainstorming is an excellent way to come up with ideas. It is important to generate as many ideas as possible – concentrate on quantity rather than quality. During the LCVP, try to absorb as many new enterprise ideas as you can and document them in an 'ideas page' in your LCVP folder or copybook.

- Decide on a product/service.
- Develop a new idea. This could be achieved by brainstorming.
- Copy an existing idea, look at competitors or get ideas from abroad.
- Change an existing idea – develop it, add something new, reduce features, etc.
- Identify a gap in the market – find a need or desire that no other company is addressing.
- Enter a niche market, i.e. a specialised market.
- Do some research and development. You could survey, interview, use the internet or contact consultants and agencies that support enterprise.

Next, you need to prioritise your ideas. Your enterprise activity must be achievable within the time constraints of the LCVP. You need to ask yourself whether the group has the necessary skills to complete this activity successfully. This is a team activity and it is essential that every member of the group can and does contribute.

You need to take the following into consideration:

- Is there a demand for this product or service?
- Will it be successful?

Tip: Have an entrepreneur from the student enterprise awards as a visitor.

Remember, the most innovative ideas do not necessarily guarantee success. Sometimes simple ideas are the most effective.

Planning Your Enterprise Activity

The enterprise activity provides you with an ideal opportunity to use an enterprise/action plan (see the template on page 6). Not only is it an excellent way to plan your enterprise activity, but it also provides you with a portfolio entry. Planning and preparing plans is also an excellent life skill because all businesses must prepare a business plan, which is similar to an enterprise/action plan.

Participating in this activity will benefit you in the following ways:

- It will force you to look at all aspects of planning.
- It helps you learn numerous skills and develop your qualities.
- It makes you be part of a team and learn all the characteristics of teamwork, which is an important skill in the world of work.
- It develops critical and lateral thinking and thinking outside the box.
- It helps you to evaluate all ideas and choose the best option.

> Once you have prepared your plan, you must be careful not to stray from it.

Running an enterprise activity will give you a greater understanding of what it is like to run a business, which is something you may consider in the future.

Ten Reasons for Establishing Your Own Business

1. **Be your own boss:** You will be your own boss and make the decisions that are important for the success or failure of your business.
2. **Pension:** You will have the opportunity to safeguard for retirement, e.g. by selling the business when you retire.
3. **Enjoyment:** You can work in an area that you enjoy and follow your passion. Therefore, working long hours doesn't really feel like work.
4. **Personal satisfaction:** It is very rewarding to create a successful business.
5. **All aspects of a business:** You will learn more about every aspect of a business and gain experience in a variety of disciplines.
6. **Work–life balance:** Owning your own business can give you a more flexible lifestyle, e.g. you may decide to work from home.
7. **Risk and reward:** You take the risks, but you also reap the rewards. You are in the driving seat and are in charge of your destiny.
8. **Connect with customers:** You get to deal with customers directly.
9. **Choose your team:** You are the boss and can hire and fire employees.
10. **Long holidays:** You can take long holidays, provided, of course, that your business will allow for it.

You need to understand the following areas. They will also help you with your enterprise.

Marketing

'Marketing' is the term used to describe **all aspects** of selling goods and services, from market research to purchasing raw materials, producing the product, selling and distributing the product or service, to after-sales service. Marketing identifies, anticipates and satisfies consumers' needs while still making a profit. Your experience of setting up and running your own enterprise will provide you with an ideal opportunity to put marketing ideas into practice.

> Market research reduces the risks associated with introducing and developing products and services.

Market research is an important element of marketing. Market research is the gathering and analysing of information related to your product/service. It is used to discover the needs and wants of customers as well as other important information. Running an enterprise activity provides you with an ideal opportunity to understand the importance of market research and to apply the marketing concept. You will need to consider the practical importance of the marketing mix by using it to sell your product or service.

Reasons for Market Research

- Market research is used to identify the types of people interested in a particular product or service.
- Market research is used to find out what potential customers need and want.
- It is used to test whether advertising is effective.
- It can help the producers to establish a suitable selling price.
- It is used to investigate competitors, i.e. to find out their strengths, weaknesses and prices.
- Market research can help determine what standard of quality the producer should try to achieve.
- It reduces the risks associated with business and helps to ensure that the business is successful.

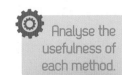

Analyse the usefulness of each method.

Types of Market Research

Desk research (secondary)	Field research (primary)

This type of research involves finding information that has already been **published**. Sources include:
 	
- Newspapers
- Central Statistics Office
- Internet
- Magazine and trade journals
- Reports from:
  – Government departments
  – Chamber of commerce
  – Local Enterprise Offices
	This type of research involves going out into the marketplace and **interviewing** customers and potential customers. It involves:
	
	- Collecting information
	- Questionnaires
	- Observation
	- Personal interviews
	- Telephone interviews
	- Consumer panels
	- Retail audits

☐ Fair
☐ Poor
☐ na

How likely are
are ...
☑ Excellent
☐ Very Goo
☐ Good
☐ Fair
☐ Poor

Usefulness of the internet

A wide variety of information can be accessed. It can be downloaded day or night. It is a cheap form of research. However, it may be difficult to filter and may not be specific to your needs.

Market Research – Questionnaires

When designing a questionnaire, be sure to include the following:

- Label your document 'questionaire'.
- Use headings and clear instructions, e.g. 'Tick the appropriate box (√)'.
- Leave a clearly marked space for answers.
- Number the questions.
- Make sure each question is clear and easy to understand.
- Keep questionnaires simple and short.
- Test out your questionnaire on a small group of people first.
- Questionnaires usually have a question on personal details and price.
- Avoid leading questions and limit open questions.

> **Tip:** What information is required? Draft suitable questions to obtain this information. Design a possible questionnaire.

Designing a Questionnaire

A questionnaire must be carefully designed in a way that is easy to understand but also has enough detail to get the required information. Before designing a questionnaire, brainstorm what information is required.

Activity

Design a questionnaire for Gorgeous Gardens. List the information required and draft appropriate questions.

Why is research important?

Research is important because it gives you the information you need and helps you to make decisions. Research helps you to identify customers' needs and wants and avoids failures and wasting time.

How to ensure the survey is successful

- The questionnaire should ask the questions you need answers for. Make sure to use the appropriate style of questions.
- The questionnaire should be easy and quick to complete.
- You should try to get a good response or sample so that it represents the total population. A sample should be representative of the total population. The bigger the sample, the more accurate the results (but the greater the costs).
- Collect information quickly and correctly.
- Properly analyse the information.

What items should be examined in evaluating the process?

- Did the LCVP class work well as a team?
- Was the brief given carried out properly?
- How well was the questionnaire drawn up?
- How well organised was the administration of the questionnaire, i.e. distribution, collection, publicity, response rate?
- Time management – how long did it take? Did you meet your deadlines?
- How were the results collated?
- Did it cause disruptions in the school?
- Were there any other problems? How did you overcome them?

Types of questions for a questionnaire

- **Dichotomous questions/closed questions/direct response questions:** This requires a simple response (e.g. Yes or No) and the answers are easy to collate.

> Please tick (✔) the appropriate box.
>
> Question: Do you like music? Yes ☐   No ☐

- **Multiple choice questions:** This requires selecting a, b, c, d or e and the answers are easy to collate.

> Please tick (✔) the appropriate box.
>
> Are you paid:
>
> (a) Weekly ☐   (b) Fortnightly ☐   (c) Monthly ☐   (d) Contract ☐   (e) Other ☐

- **Open-ended questions:** The respondent has a chance to give his or her own opinion. These answers are difficult to collate, but are extremely informative. Ideally, you should have one open-ended question in your questionnaire.

> What do you think about our product?
>
> _____
>
> _____

Remember, one very important aspect of conducting a survey is designing the **right questions**.

Carefully word all questions so that they are easy to understand.

Sample questionnaire

Questionnaire
Gorgeous Gardens Ltd
Athlumny Road, Navan

Garden Furniture

Please tick (✓) the appropriate box.

Tip: This could be an examination question.

1. Are you:

Male ☐

Female ☐

2. Which age group are you in?
(a) 20–35 ☐   (b) 36–55 ☐   (c) 56+ ☐   (d) Other ☐

3. Would you buy garden furniture?
Yes ☐   No ☐

4. Which type of garden furniture would you be interested in purchasing?
Garden Swing ☐   Picnic Table ☐   Garden Bench ☐   Other ☐

(please specify) _____

5. Which finish would you prefer on your garden furniture?
Dark ☐   Mahogany ☐   Medium Dark ☐   Chestnut Brown ☐
Light Green ☐   Other ☐

(please specify) _____

6. How much would you be willing to spend on garden furniture?
€200–€300 ☐   €301–€400 ☐   €401–€500 ☐   Other ☐

7. Any other comments? _____

_____

Thank you for taking the time to complete our questionnaire.

Identify the **type of questions** in the above questionnaire. Once you have designed your questionnaire, you must then decide how you will distribute it, e.g. by post, telephone, e-mail or by interviewing. You must also decide on the number of people you wish to survey (which is called the sample).

The Marketing Mix

The marketing mix is about getting the four Ps (product, price, place and promotion – and sometimes packaging and personnel too) correct in order to successfully sell the product or service.

Marketing Mix – The Four Ps

Product	■ Produce the right product or service. ■ Design the product or service to suit consumer needs and wants. ■ Ensure excellent quality. ■ Develop an ideal brand and promote an outstanding image, e.g. Apple. ■ Ensure the packaging enhances the product and is appropriate. ■ Having a unique selling point (USP) ensures your product or service has a competitive advantage.
Price	■ Choose the most suitable price, depending on the product. ■ You must cover all costs and yield a sufficient profit. ■ The price may be determined by demand for the product or service. ■ You must take competitors' price into account. ■ Prices may change from time to time, e.g. during sales.
Place	■ Identify your market and choose the best way to distribute your product or service. There are different ways of getting the product or service from you to the consumer: – Manufacturer – wholesale – retailer – customer – Manufacturer – wholesale – customer – Manufacturer – customer
Promotion	■ Choose the most appropriate promotion techniques to increase or encourage sales. ■ Use sales promotions – these are gimmicks used to encourage customers to buy products or services, e.g. 10% extra free, special offers, loyalty cards and points. ■ Advertise in newspapers, on the internet, on the radio or on the TV, making sure that you reach your target market. ■ Personal selling (e.g. salespeople) can be effective. ■ Public relations (PR) promotes awareness of the product to the general public.

Package and personnel may also be identified as additional Ps in the marketing mix.

Tip: Look up a YouTube video on the marketing mix.

Marketing Mix Case Study

Case Study – Myona Music

Myona Music is a successful enterprise that was established by two highly motivated and enterprising students from Presentation De La Salle College, Bagenalstown, Co. Carlow. Amy Ryan and Rhona McGarvey are the two people who set up Myona Music.

Their innovative idea was to produce a music booklet with an accompanying CD. All of the songs on the CD can be played at a slow or normal speed, enabling people to learn to read, listen and play the tin whistle. The idea was based on both the Suzuki method (listening and playing by ear) and the classical method (reading music notes) for the tin whistle.

Myona Music's success was due to their excellent marketing. They did extensive market research and identified a niche (gap) in the market. They devised a marketing strategy to create a product and service to win over their customers, who were both teachers and students.

They carefully put together the right marketing mix of product, price, place, promotion and personnel.

The product was a music booklet with accompanying CD, while the service consisted of workshops that could be arranged to enhance the learning of music. The price was decided on after extensive market research. The price was determined by the unit cost, the level of demand, the competition and the target market. The price varied from €15.00 to €20.00, with bulk discounts.

Due to the nature of the product and service, they sold it in the following places: craft fairs, primary schools, newsletters and through their website. They used every opportunity to promote their product and service, e.g. launches, leaflets, window displays. They came up with a brand name, Myona Music, and then developed a brand image using their local GAA colours, yellow and black, in their promotional activities. The personnel involved two students who were enthusiastic about music and who combined their hobby (music) with an enterprise activity. They also created 'Myona Music's top ten tips' for learning the tin whistle, reminding people that practice makes perfect! They opted for a clear packaging so that potential customers could see their booklet and CD.

Their success was due to their extensive and ongoing market research.

Using the above case study, document the marketing mix for Myona Music.

Promotion

Promotion encourages customers to buy goods and services. There are basically four methods of promotion: personal selling, advertising, sales promotion and public relations. The combination of these methods is called the promotional mix.

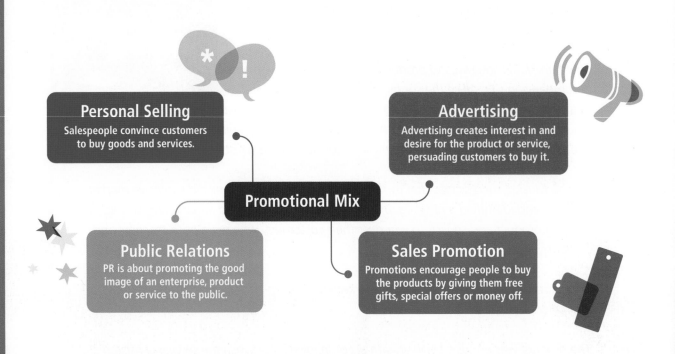

Personal Selling
Salespeople convince customers to buy goods and services.

Advertising
Advertising creates interest in and desire for the product or service, persuading customers to buy it.

Promotional Mix

Public Relations
PR is about promoting the good image of an enterprise, product or service to the public.

Sales Promotion
Promotions encourage people to buy the products by giving them free gifts, special offers or money off.

Advertising

Advertising communicates information about a product or service, with a view to persuading customers and potential customers to buy it.

Reasons for advertising

- Advertising attracts attention.
- It inspires interest.
- It develops a desire for the produce or service.
- It achieves action, i.e. it persuades the customer to actually buy the product or service.

Forms of advertising

- Social media
- Television
- Radio
- Magazines
- Newspapers

- Cinema
- Billboards
- Shopping bags
- Sponsorship
- Competitions

Discuss all forms of advertising as a class discussion.

Planning an advertising campaign

When planning an advertising campaign, it is important to:

- Have clear objectives or aims.
- Decide on a budget.
- Choose an appropriate form of advertising.
- Decide on an advertising agency or appoint an advertising manager.

Remember, advertising will only be successful if your campaign is carefully planned.

After the campaign, **evaluate** it to see:

- What worked well?
- What aspects were cost effective?
- What would you do differently? Apply the DAR approach (see page 15).

How can you **evaluate**?

- Identify the costs involved to see if the campaign was effective.
- Survey the public.
- Check if sales have shown a significant increase.
- Ask employees for their opinions.

Activity

Plan an advertising campaign for an organisation of your choice. Use an enterprise/action plan template.

As part of this unit you are encouraged to plan, run and evaluate an enterprise activity as a **team**. This can be recorded in an enterprise report.

Enterprise Report Guidelines

Tip: 1,000–1,500 words.

Title page	■ **Title:** An LCVP Enterprise Activity ■ **Subtitle:** To ensure greater detail, perhaps a learning outcome ■ **Author's name:** Your name ■ **Intended audience:** For the attention of the Link Modules teacher ■ **Date of completion:** Ensure it is within the two years of the LCVP, e.g. March 2015
Table of contents	■ This is a list of the main elements or sections of the report, giving the page numbers on which they appear. All pages must be numbered.

Summary	■ This paragraph should include appropriate information, such as:
	  – The subject of the report
	  – The main items dealt with in the text
	  – The main conclusions and recommendations

Terms of reference OR aims	■ Why the report was written or requested ■ What you or the group hoped to learn or achieve from the activity
Body of the report	■ Key details of the enterprise activity are described ■ Write paragraphs in a logical sequence under clear headings (and subheadings as appropriate). ■ Relevant information, such as idea generation, research undertaken, plans made, actions agreed and tasks carried out, should be recorded accurately and concisely. ■ The conclusions must refer back to the body of the report, so it is important to present the body of the report in a logical sequence. **Apply the learning cycle: PEP** ■ Include a financial element (some revenue and costs). ■ You should include at least one relevant illustration to support the main findings of the report, e.g. a small table, diagram or chart. **Evidence of your personal contribution (choose one)** ■ Include a paragraph titled 'My Personal Contribution' in the body of the report. This is probably the most popular and easiest option. ■ Highlight your personal contribution (e.g. by using *italics*) at appropriate points in the text. ■ Include an overview and evaluation of your personal contribution at the end of the document.

Conclusions	▪ Should relate to the body of the report and link to the rationale of LCVP.
Recommendations	▪ Ensure recommendations are based on the report's conclusions (e.g. suggestions for future action). Be sure to elaborate and discuss skills.
Evaluation	▪ Include an evaluation of the following: – The enterprise activity itself, while linking to the objectives – Group performance – revise teamwork – If not dealt with separately, an evaluation of your personal performance
Appendices	▪ Maximum two items to support the main findings of the enterprise report ▪ Cross-reference them in the main report (e.g. Appendix 1) ▪ Material you could include in an appendix are: – Photographs of products/exhibitions/meetings – Charts, e.g. sales and costs – Diagrams – Detailed accounts

Tip: Teamwork in LCVP: means working with others to generate ideas, appreciating the value of teamwork, actively participating in the group and assessing group skills.

Before you start to write the enterprise report, revise the following:

- **Planning:** How to plan, why plan, business plan, advantages of planning.
- **Skills/qualities:** Define, explain and give examples.
- **Teamwork:** Define, advantages, disadvantages, skills required by members.
- **Idea generation, research, marketing and advertising.**
- **Evaluation:** How? Why? Where? Who? When?
- **Specific learning outcomes (SLOs)** relating to Enterprise Education in the Link Modules.

Document a detailed enterprise report, which will help you prepare for the written paper. You may decide to submit your enterprise activity report as a summary report instead of a detailed enterprise report.

Follow the ten tips on how to perfect your portfolio on pages 190–91.

Tip: All portfolio items must be consistent. See the tips on page 191.

Enterprise Report Template

Use the following template to start your report writing in your LCVP folder or copybook.

Title:

Tip: This is just a draft template to help you start your report.

Subtitle:

Author's name:

For the attention of:

Date:

Table of contents:

Summary:

Aims:

Body of report:

Conclusions:

Recommendations:

Evaluation:

   Activity:

   Group performance:

Appendices (maximum 2 items)
1.

2.

Tip: Make sure to cross-reference appendix items.

Tip: When actually drafting your report, use **bold** only for headings.

Checklist for success criteria for the enterprise report

When you have finished your enterprise report, read the list below to make sure you fulfil the LCVP requirements. Be sure to elaborate and articulate the learning for each portfolio item. Go to Section 4: Assessment to check general rules for the portfolio and apply the ten tips for perfecting your portfolio items on pages 190–91.

- ✓ Is your enterprise report word-processed?
- ✓ Have you checked that your word count is between 1,000 and 1,500 words?
- ✓ Does your enterprise report relate to an LCVP enterprise that you engaged in during the course of the two-year programme? Remember, you can't use your transition year enterprise.
- ✓ Have you been consistent in your use of punctuation, capitals, grammar, font, underlining, etc.?
- ✓ Do you have a clear title stating that it is an enterprise report?
- ✓ Have you included a subtitle that describes the activity with extra detail?
- ✓ Did you state your name as the author?
- ✓ Have you included 'for the attention of' and the date of completion (which must be some time during the two years of LCVP)?
- ✓ Have you included a table of contents?
- ✓ Have you numbered the pages and recorded these numbers in the table of contents?
- ✓ Have you included a summary that gives a synopsis of the enterprise report?
- ✓ Have you stated at least five aims (both group and personal)?
- ✓ Is the report based on a group activity?
- ✓ Have you described your personal contribution (a paragraph) to the enterprise activity?
- ✓ Have you arranged the report in a logical sequence (especially the body of the report), with clear headings and subheadings?
- ✓ Have you included illustrations or tables?
- ✓ Have you described the financial impact of the enterprise activity and included some accounts?
- ✓ Did you give at least three conclusions that relate to the body of the enterprise report?
- ✓ Resulting from the conclusions you have come to, did you make recommendations?
- ✓ Have you evaluated the experience of the enterprise activity and to what extent you achieved your aims?
- ✓ Have you evaluated the group performance of the enterprise activity?
- ✓ Have you evaluated your individual performance of the enterprise activity?
- ✓ Did you submit an appendix with a maximum of two items, including a chart, diagram or picture to support the main findings?
- ✓ Proofread your enterprise report to make sure it is free of errors and as perfect as possible.

Work in pairs and use this checklist to evaluate your portfolio. Ask for explanations.

Mind Map: Outline of an Enterprise Report

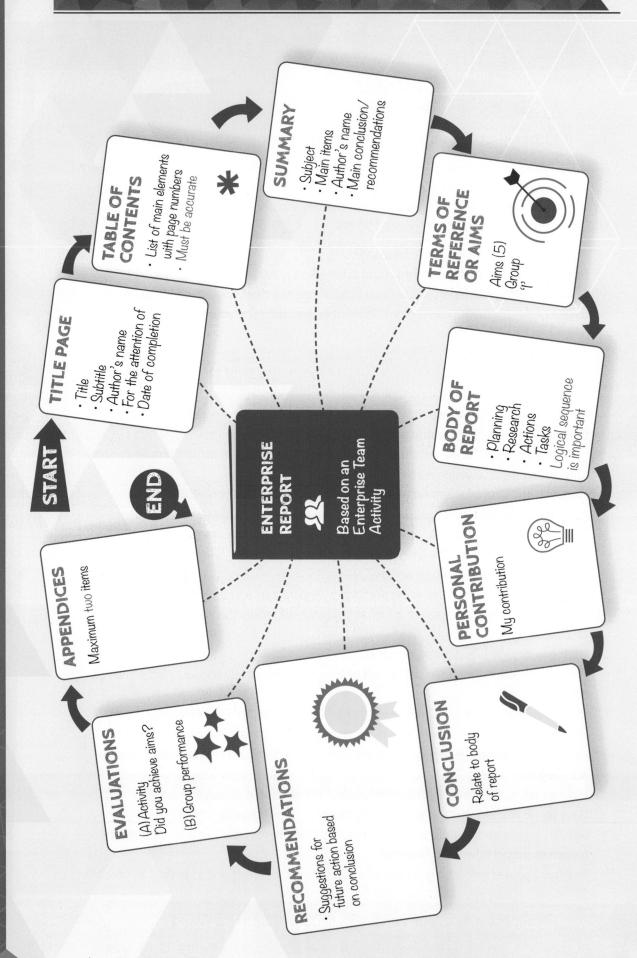

SUMMARY
- Subject
- Main items
- Author's name
- Main conclusion/ recommendations

TABLE OF CONTENTS
- List of main elements with page numbers
- Must be accurate

TERMS OF REFERENCE OR AIMS
Aims (5)
Group '?'

TITLE PAGE
- Title
- Subtitle
- Author's name
- For the attention of
- Date of completion

START

END

ENTERPRISE REPORT
Based on an Enterprise Team Activity

BODY OF REPORT
- Planning
- Research
- Actions
- Tasks
Logical sequence is important

APPENDICES
Maximum two items

PERSONAL CONTRIBUTION
My contribution

EVALUATIONS
(A) Activity
Did you achieve aims?
(B) Group performance

RECOMMENDATIONS
- Suggestions for future action based on conclusion

CONCLUSION
Relate to body of report

Sample Portfolio Item

ENTERPRISE REPORT

ENTERPRISE REPORT

An LCVP enterprise activity to raise money to
subsidise the cost of school sports gear

Author:

For the attention

Date:

Summary
The following is a report on a fundraiser organised by LCVP students. The report outlines the aims and
objectives, planning and organisation of this enterprise activity. After extensive research we
decided on an activity to subsidise the cost of sports gear for our school. We decided
to raise money for both a hurling and a football all-star team. We achieved our aims and
the activity was definitely a success as we and raised more money than we could have
anticipated. Research, careful planning and immense organisation were all contributing
factors to this as an excellent enterprise activity.

- **Market research**
  We decided to engage in research to ensure sufficient interest amongst students to partake in the activity.
  I undertook the challenge of market research. I drew up a questionnaire and distributed it amongst a
  sample of students. I then gathered, recorded and analysed all the information that I had received. This
  information showed us that there was a phenomenal amount of interest among the students.
- **Web research**
  We also researched suppliers using the internet.

Preparation
- **Preparing nominee cards**
  We downloaded the sports all-star nominee cards from the
  numbered each card and organised them into bundles of 2
- **Contacting sports gear retailers**
  We wrote letters to various sports gear retailers requesting
  companies and also an offer to send a representative
  this offer and arrange

- Buy a jacket for €50 – sell 25 cards @ €2
- Buy shorts and socks for €30 – sell 15 cards @ €2
- Buy the jacket, shorts and socks for €70 – sell 35 cards @ €2

for both instead of €80, as this would act as an incentive.
to bring in €30 for shorts and socks, and if they could not sell the nominees
themselves. The jacket success and are a fashion item worn by

Table of contents   **Page**

- Sum
- Terms of Referen
- Aims and Object
- Planning
- Researching
- Preparation
- Organisation
- My Personal C
- Conclusions
- Recommenda
- Evaluation
- Appendices

The team was a major contributing factor to the success of this enterprise activity. We worked well as a
team by using our interpersonal and intrapersonal skills to ensure we made our own personal contribution
while also working as a team during the activity.
There were some disagreements along the way, but we learned to overcome them. I feel that these were
important, as by resolving them mix the ideas and opinions of different people to attain the
best results possible. Resolving closer together, as we worked
together to see each other's
our team, better known as
I also developed skills to in
fy my point of view while
vitae and hopefully help m

could decide what sizes they
their orders.

culate the winners. We calculated

Appendix
1.1

Sports gear
1.2

Appendices

1.1

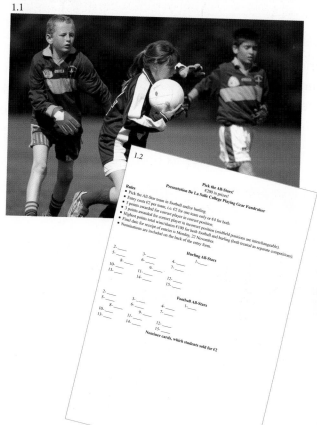

1.2

Pick the All-Stars!
€200 in prizes!
Presentation De La Salle College Playing Gear Fundraiser

Rules
- Pick the All-Star team in football and/or hurling.
- Entry costs €2 per team, i.e. €2 for one team only or €4 for both.
- 5 points awarded for correct player in correct position.
- 3 points awarded for correct player in incorrect position (midfield positions are interchangeable).
- Highest points total wins/shares €100 for both football and hurling (both treated as separate competitions).
- Final date for receipt of entries is Monday, 22 November.
- Nominations are included on the back of the entry form.

Hurling All-Stars
1. ___
2. ___   3. ___
5. ___
8. ___   6. ___   7. ___
10. ___   9. ___
13. ___   11. ___   12. ___
14. ___
15. ___

Football All-Stars
1. ___
2. ___   3. ___
5. ___
8. ___   6. ___   7. ___
10. ___   9. ___
13. ___   11. ___   12. ___
14. ___
15. ___

Nominee cards, which students sold for €2

Learning Board

Key Questions

Answer these questions in your LCVP folder or copybook.
1. Briefly summarise the main points using key words from the unit.
2. Write down something you learned.
3. Write down something you found difficult or challenging.

Devise an Exam Question

Write three exam questions in your LCVP folder or copybook. Start with a quotation, perhaps a specific learning outcome (SLO) or a sentence from this unit.

Presentation

Write a **six-sentence presentation** on the marketing mix. This can be an individual attempt or work in teams to create a presentation.

Portfolio

Can I use this for my **portfolio**?   Yes ☐   No ☐
The portfolio is worth 60%.

If yes:

CORE – submit all 4
→ Curriculum vitae
→ Enterprise/action plan
→ Career investigation
→ Summary report

OPTIONAL – submit 2 out of 4
→ Diary of work experience
→ Enterprise report
→ Report on 'My Own Place'
→ Recorded interview/presentation

A total of six portfolio items must be submitted.

Skills

Now that you have worked through this unit, what are the next steps?
What new skills have you acquired? Describe them.

Tasks

1. Explain the term 'market research'.
2. Discuss advertising and promotions.
3. Describe successes and problems encountered in your enterprise activity.
4. List advice and consultants available for your enterprise activity.
5. Describe the promotional mix.
6. Discuss the marketing mix and apply this to a product of your choice.
7. Discuss the planning you engaged in while participating in your enterprise activity.
8. Did you discover any useful websites/YouTube clips?

Learning Board

> **Tip:** Revisit after completing all units.

Cross-curricular

Cross-curricular refers to activities or themes that are relevant to many subjects across the curriculum. For example, health and safety is important in Chemistry, Construction Studies, Engineering, Home Economics and Business.

Answer the following in your LCVP folder or copybook.

1. What Leaving Certificate subjects were useful?
2. How were they useful?
3. Were your vocational subject groupings (VSGs) useful?

Learning Outcomes

Revisit the specific learning outcomes on page 165.
Do you understand each SLO?

Key Words

Do you understand the key words on page 165? Write three sentences on each word.

Key Examination Words

Do you understand the key examination words on page 208? For all the main themes, you will need to demonstrate a deep understanding by:

- Describing the term
- Explaining the term
- Demonstrating the term
- Illustrating the term
- Differentiating the term
- Evaluating the term

> **Tip:** This links with Bloom's taxonomy.

Evidence

You will need to show evidence of your learning. It is your responsibility to keep draft copies of your work. It is a good idea to label and date all activities and handouts in your copy or LCVP folder.

> **Tip:** Draft a mind map to demonstrate learning in this unit.

Twenty Sample Questions

The questions on page 185 can first be attempted orally, followed by written answers.

> **Tip:** To improve your examination performance, you need to practise.

Making It Happen:
Preparing for Assessment

Assessment ideas based on Enterprise Education
Unit 4 – An Enterprise Activity

Portfolio of coursework: 60%

Core

→ **Enterprise/action plan**
  – Plan an enterprise activity
→ **Summary report**
  – An enterprise activity (provided you don't submit an enterprise report in the options)

Options

→ **Enterprise report**
→ **Recorded interview/presentation**
  – General interview: one or two questions on your enterprise activity

Written paper: 40%

→ **Revise** the following:
  – Idea generation
  – Training needs
  – Recruiting consultants
  – Market research
  – Designing a questionnaire
  – Marketing mix
  – Publicity and promotion
  – Teamwork
  – How targets are reached

⚙ Revise the layout and content of your portfolio items.

→ **Prepare** for questions that demonstrate you participated in an activity, e.g. visit in, visit out. Don't forget to use the PEP approach: pre-experience, experience, post-experience. Part of the learning cycle of the LCVP is planning, participating and evaluating.

→ **Cross-curricular learning** – what Leaving Certificate subjects were useful and how were they useful, in particular your vocational subject groupings (VSGs).

→ **Analyse** your individual contribution and personal performance.

→ **Evaluation** involves looking at and judging the quality of the enterprise activity and asking yourself if you achieved your goals. Consider the following:
  – How and why do we evaluate?
  – Evaluate your enterprise activity.
  – Evaluate group performance/teamwork.

Twenty Sample Questions

1. Your LCVP class is planning an enterprise activity to sell refill pads and pens. Design a suitable questionnaire.

Tip: In the examination, a question will normally have four parts. Revise examination preparation.

2. Describe an enterprise activity you participated in as part of the LCVP.

3. Why would a business engage in training?

4. Why is research important for a business?

5. Identify a product you wish to promote and design an advertising campaign for it.

6. List **five** methods of generating ideas and describe **one** method in detail.

7. Draft a business plan for an enterprise of your choice.

8. Discuss how you can evaluate your enterprise activity.

9. Why would you evaluate the **organisation** of an enterprise activity?

10. Describe the benefits of participating in an LCVP enterprise activity.

11. Compare desk research with field research.

12. How can you evaluate an advertising campaign?

13. Discuss the challenges facing businesses.

14. Explain the term 'marketing mix'. Apply the marketing mix to an enterprise you participated in as part of the LCVP.

15. Identify a problem you encountered when participating in your enterprise activity and outline how you overcame the problem.

16. Name Leaving Certificate subjects that helped you with your enterprise activity and give reasons for your choices.

17. Describe what makes a business successful.

18. Outline how you would organise an enterprise activity.

19. Complete a SWOT analysis of your LCVP enterprise.

20. Outline enterprise qualities and skills.

Tip: Skim Section 4: Assessment, in particular the section on revising exam questions (pages 202–205).

Assessment

Finally, we must prepare for assessment. This section offers additional guidelines and practical advice. **Keep a copy of your portfolio and use it as a revision tool for the written paper.** Read through your portfolio the night before the written paper examination, and if you get a chance, read it again the morning of the exam. Your portfolio will help you answer some of the questions, so make sure that you are very familiar with the **content** and the **layout** of each of the portfolio items.

Overview of Assessment

The **two** Link Modules (Preparation for the World of Work and Enterprise Education) are treated as one unit for assessment purposes and the assessment is at a **common level**. Upon completion of the programme you must present **evidence** in relation to the specific learning outcomes (SLOs).

Tip: It is important to revise and prepare for the assessment. The PEP approach in this book will help you prepare.

LCVP Assessment

Written examination paper – 40% of total marks (160/400)

Date	End of final year of the LCVP	First Wednesday in May of the final year of the LCVP	
Duration	2.5 hours		
Content	Section A	Audio-visual presentation	30
	Section B	Case study (received in advance)	30
	Section C	General questions	100
		(4 x 25 marks – answer 4 out of 6)	
TOTAL MARKS			160

Tip: It is important to practise questions.

Portfolio of coursework – 60% of total marks (240/400)

Date	Assessed at the end of the final year of the LCVP	Submit on the first Wednesday in March of the final year of the LCVP	
Duration	Assembled over two years of the programme		
Content	1. **Core items**	Curriculum vitae	25
	All 4 items to be presented	Enterprise/action plan	35
		Career investigation	40
		Summary report	40
	2. **Optional items**	Diary of work experience	50
	2 out of 4 items to be presented	Enterprise report	50
		Report on 'My Own Place'	50
		Recorded interview/presentation	50
TOTAL MARKS			240

Tip: Your portfolio should be perfect and free of errors.

TOTAL MARKS: 400 (for both the written exam and portfolio)

Structure of Link Modules examination 40%

Section A
Audio-visual presentation: 30 marks
Students answer all 8 questions

Section B
Case study: 30 marks
Students answer all 3 questions

Section C
General questions: 100 marks
Students answer 4 out of 6 questions

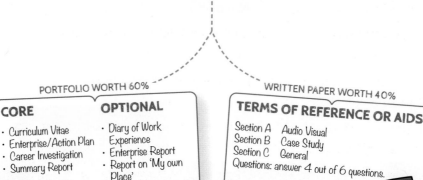

ASSESSMENT

PORTFOLIO WORTH 60%

CORE
· Curriculum Vitae
· Enterprise/Action Plan
· Career Investigation
· Summary Report

OPTIONAL
· Diary of Work Experience
· Enterprise Report
· Report on 'My own Place'
· Recorded Interview/ Presentation

ENSURE TO FOLLOW GUIDELINES

WRITTEN PAPER WORTH 40%

TERMS OF REFERENCE OR AIDS
Section A   Audio Visual
Section B   Case Study
Section C   General
Questions: answer 4 out of 6 questions.

PRACTICE PAST EXAMINATION QUESTIONS

BOTH MODULES ARE TREATED AS ONE FOR ASSESSMENT PURPOSES.
LINK THE LEARNING TO THE RELEVANT LEAVING CERTIFICATE SUBJECTS.

Certification

LCVP students receive the same certificate as Leaving Certificate students. An additional statement of the grade received for the Link Modules is applied to the certificate. Grades for the Link Modules are awarded as follows:

- **Distinction (80–100%)**
- **Merit (65–79%)**
- **Pass (50–64%)**

Points

LCVP students have the same opportunity to proceed to universities and other third-level institutions as Leaving Certificate students. The Link Modules are presently recognised in points terms at universities and institutes of technology as follows:

- **Distinction: 70 points**
- **Merit: 50 points**
- **Pass: 30 points**

The State Examinations Commission issues guidelines each year that highlight any changes in assessment.

Portfolio of Coursework

A portfolio is a purposeful collection of your work that exhibits your efforts, progress and achievements. The purpose of the LCVP portfolio is to demonstrate the depth and breadth of your skills and capabilities through examples of your work. The portfolio is generated over a two-year period and you are encouraged to revisit and revise your work. It should represent a collection of your **best work**. It must be prepared in accordance with specific criteria and provide evidence that you have planned and participated in and learned from a variety of activities organised as part of the Link Modules. The content of the portfolio must relate to the syllabus, in particular the specific learning outcomes (SLOs), and must be presented according to assessment criteria and important guidelines.

You must submit **six pieces** of work for the LCVP portfolio. This counts for 60% of your final mark in the Link Modules.

There are **four** compulsory core items: a curriculum vitae, an enterprise/action plan, a career investigation and a summary report.

You must also submit any **two** of the four optional items: a diary of work experience, an enterprise report, a 'My Own Place' report and a recorded interview or presentation.

> Follow the success criteria. However, you have to articulate skills and make sure your work is error free – perfect.

Portfolio of coursework (60%)	
Compulsory core items (all 4)	■ Curriculum vitae ■ Enterprise/action plan ■ Career investigation ■ Summary report
Options (any 2)	■ Diary of work experience ■ Enterprise report ■ 'My Own Place' report ■ Recorded interview/presentation

> It is your responsibility to select items to include in your portfolio, which must be your own work.

Your teacher will tell you about any changes in guidelines issued by the examining authority. You should also look at the chief advising examiner's reports.

Portfolio Restrictions

The following portfolio restrictions are outlined in the LCVP guidelines.

- You cannot have any **duplication**.
- You may not submit a summary report on a career investigation.
- If you submit an enterprise report in the options, you cannot submit a summary report on the same activity.
- If you submit a 'My Own Place' report in the options, you cannot submit a summary report on the same activity.
- If you submit a diary of work experience in the options, you cannot submit a summary report on the same activity.

- If you submit a recorded interview/presentation, you cannot submit a summary report on the same activity.
- However, you may prepare an enterprise/action plan for any activity already reported on in the portfolio, provided the plan is not reproduced in that report or diary.
- The content of the career investigation, summary report or any other optional item may not be the main topic of your recorded interview/presentation. An activity you have already reported on should not account for more than 25% of the recorded interview.

Remember, **the portfolio is exam material** and the integrity of the examination process must be protected. You must produce your own items for the portfolio. Any examples are only a guide to style, not to content. Your results can be withheld if work presented is too similar to examples. However, if you follow guidelines and participate in the activities, this will ensure good portfolio items.

Portfolio Content

- You must only submit material generated as a result of Link Modules activities in which you participated over the two years of the LCVP. Work experience that you participated in during transition year is not accepted.
- Only submit **six items**.
- Each item must be your own original work. Keep drafts of all your work.
- Including material directly downloaded or copied from other sources is not acceptable.
- Portfolio items should relate to a number of separate activities.

Ten Tips for Perfecting Your Portfolio Items

1. Marks will be awarded for presentation. You will be tested on your word-processing, design and composition skills as well as on the content of your portfolio items.
2. The portfolio must be your own work and represent your individual effort. Be sure to record a personal objective, personal research methods and personal evaluation and articulate numerous personal skills developed as a result of the LCVP.
3. The portfolio items must be generated as a result of the Link Modules only and must relate to a number of different LCVP activities. All activities must link to an SLO.
4. Include your Leaving Certificate examination number on the cover of the LCVP portfolio. Use spine-bound A4 white paper with no plastic-covered pages.
5. Times New Roman font, size 12, is recommended. Use size 14 and bold for headings.
6. You have two years to complete your portfolio entries. Check them carefully – they should be free of errors. Double-check the following:
   - Consistent font
   - No spelling mistakes
   - Consistent layout, with headings all the same size and style (e.g. size 14, bold)
   - Grammar and punctuation are perfect
   - Consistent spacing, always one stop after a full stop. Use tables when appropriate.
   - Correct word count

Tip: Consistency within portfolio items is very important.

7. Include a contents page with the list of core items (curriculum vitae, enterprise/action plan, career investigation and summary report) and optional items (diary of work experience, enterprise report, the 'My Own Place' report and the recorded interview/presentation). Arrange the portfolio items in the order of the LCVP marking scheme.

8. Place an insert page in front of each item with its title on it, e.g. Curriculum Vitae, and then the portfolio item itself.

9. Remember to link your activities to the World of Work, Enterprise Education and third level. Be specific – for example, if you mention a relevant Leaving Certificate subject in the diary of work experience, be sure to mention the course too. Always elaborate and give an example.

10. Apply the PEP approach (pre-experience, experience, post-experience) to activities and document them in a logical way.

> **All portfolio items must be consistent:**
> - Use one space after a full stop.
> - All headings should be set in bold and Times New Roman size 14. Use size 12 for the rest of the text.
> - Use tabs to indent.
> - Make sure your grammar is correct and there are no spelling mistakes.
> - Make sure not to use abbreviations.
> - Use bullet points and numbering consistently. If you use numbers (1, 2, 3) after a heading, you must continue to use numbers after all headings. If you use bullet points, you must continue to use them under every heading.

> Follow the checklist for success criteria for all portfolio items.

Portfolio: Comparison of Reports

Summary report (core) 300–600 words	Enterprise report (optional) 1,000–1,500 words	'My Own Place' report (optional) 1,000–1,500 words
Title Author	Title page Title Author Intended audience Date of completion (within the 2 years of the LCVP)	Title page Title Author Intended audience Date of completion (within the 2 years of the LCVP)
	Table of contents List of main sections Page numbers	Table of contents List of main sections Page numbers
	Summary (synopsis)	Introduction: description, aspect, map
Terms of reference or aims Group ('we') and personal ('I')	Terms of reference or aims Group ('we') and personal ('I')	Terms of reference or aims Group ('we') and personal ('I')
Body Short sentences Short paragraphs Headings, subheadings Bullet points Chronological order May contain tabulated information	Body Key details of enterprise Headings, subheadings Bullet points Relevant illustrations (at least one) Evidence of personal contribution	Body Main findings of investigation Headings, subheadings Bullet points Relevant illustrations Evidence of personal contribution Out-of-school activity described Three research methods Local issue analysed Link learning to at least two Leaving Certificate subjects
Conclusions: relate to aims Recommendations: based on conclusions	Conclusions: relate to body Recommendations: based on conclusions	Conclusions: relate to aims Recommendations: based on conclusions
	Evaluation: Activity Group performance	Evaluation: Investigation Group performance
No appendices	Appendices (max. two items)	Appendices (max. two items)

The Recorded Interview/Presentation

An interview is an opportunity to show your talents. The LCVP recorded interview is a three- to five-minute interview presented on a DVD.

The recorded interview/presentation may take a variety of forms:

- A general interview – based on participation and insights gained through the Link Modules.
- A simulated job interview – it must include at least three LCVP activities.
- A short presentation (supported by simple visual aids) based on an activity you participated in, followed by two or three questions based on content.

Recorded Interview/Presentation Restrictions

- The content of a career investigation, summary report or any other optional item submitted as part of your portfolio cannot be the main topic of your recorded interview or presentation.
- As a general rule, an activity already submitted in your portfolio should not account for more than 25% of the recorded interview. In other words, your interview should represent a number of different LCVP activities.

Recorded Interview

Pre-interview

- Watch previous LCVP interviews.
- Research and prepare questions. Practise your answers.
- Be aware of the SLOs and have examples of how you achieved them ready.
- Make sure that the questions you are asked give you a chance to talk about your strengths.
- Be aware of the assessment criteria.
- Be aware of the guidelines and marking scheme.
- Make sure that the interviewer has your questions and that if he or she is not your teacher, that he or she is familiar with the LCVP Link Modules.

It is a good idea to leave the recorded interview until sixth year to ensure you can articulate all your learning and show evidence of the skills you have developed.

During the interview

- Make sure that the location is suitable – you will need a quiet room with good lighting. Make sure that the school bell is switched off.
- Communicate positively and confidently.
- Maintain eye contact with the interviewer at all times.
- Use positive body language – don't slouch or fold your arms. Try to appear open and relaxed. Don't forget to smile!
- Make sure that you are dressed neatly and appropriately.
- The recording must be at least three minutes and no more than five minutes.
- Start recording only after sitting down.
- Display your Leaving Certificate examination number at all times.
- Place the camera on a tripod and use an external microphone.

Post-interview

- Watch your performance.
- Check that your Leaving Certificate examination number can be seen at all times.
- See if there is anything you can improve on.
- Check if there are any additional points you would like to make in the interview.
- Go through the scoring sheet on page 196 and the assessment criteria.

Be aware of non-verbal communication. This is communicating through body language and tone of voice. Sometimes **how you say something** is more important than **what you say**.

Keep to the time. **Minimum** of **three minutes** and a **maximum** of **five minutes**.

Recorded Interview/Presentation Template

The following are possible interview questions for a **general interview**. A general interview must be based on participation and insights gained through the Link Modules.

Tell me about yourself.
What do you hope to do after the Leaving Certificate?
Tell me about your work experience in LCVP.
What are the main differences between work and school?
How will LCVP help you in third level or work?
When did you work in a team in LCVP? What did you learn about teams?
What do you understand by enterprise?
Tell me about some other activities you participated in during the LCVP.

The success of an interview depends on the type of questions asked.

- You may decide to develop your own questions.
- Role-play with the above interview questions.
- Use score sheets.
- Ask yourself how you can improve.

Score Sheet for a Recorded Interview/Presentation

Copy the following practice score sheet into your LCVP folder or copybook and rate your recorded interview/presentation.

	Rating (1–10)	Comment
Clear		
Fluent		
Eye contact		
Gestures		
Humour		
Structure		
Voice		
Appearance		
Posture		
Elaborate		
Link to SLOs		
Pace		
Communication		
Content		
Logical sequence		
Confident		
Informed opinions		
Personal examples		
Variety of tone		
Wrap-up		
Overall rating	/ 200	

In pairs, use the above template to comment on your interview.

Recorded Interview/Presentation Guidelines

The NCCA guidelines recommend the following when preparing for a recorded interview/presentation.

The student interviewee/presenter should:

- Dress neatly and appropriately
- Adopt an open, relaxed posture
- Make eye contact with the interviewer/audience
- Listen carefully and affirm questions with appropriate body language
- Speak clearly and confidently using a normal conversational voice
- Express ideas/opinions/points in a logical sequence
- Take care not to drop their voice at the end of sentences
- Avoid reading from notes or from visual aids
- Avoid distracting mannerisms, jargon and slang
- Explain technical terms that may be unfamiliar to the interviewer or audience
- Use hand gestures where appropriate
- Use action words and phrases when describing events (e.g. I planned, we evaluated)
- Make reference to skills gained through Link Module activities

The interviewer(s) should:

- Be familiar with the aims and expected outcomes of the Link Modules
- Plan key questions to provide structure and direction to the interview
- Avoid complex or ambiguous questions (e.g. What subjects are you studying at school? Why did you choose them? Which is your favourite?)
- Articulate questions clearly
- Adapt questions to the level of the student's abilities
- Use open questions (e.g. Tell me about…, Why do you think…)
- Encourage students to give examples and express their opinions
- Give students time to think after they are questioned
- Follow up on students' responses
- Avoid dominating the interview

Tip: A documentary-style video recording in which you act as a narrator is not recommended, as it is unlikely to satisfy the assessment criteria.

Remember, an LCVP recorded interview/presentation must relate to LCVP activities and demonstrate what you learned and the skills you developed and apply to the World of Work and Enterprise Education.

Checklist for success criteria for the recorded interview/presentation

When you have finished your recorded interview/presentation, read the list below to make sure you fulfil the LCVP requirements.

- ✓ Have you researched your LCVP recorded interview questions and prepared sample answers that demonstrate activities and skills?
- ✓ Did you start by stating your Leaving Certificate number? Did you display your Leaving Certificate exam number at all times?
- ✓ Is the interview or presentation at least three minutes and no more than five minutes?
- ✓ Does your recorded interview relate to at least **three** LCVP activities that you engaged in during the course of the two-year programme?
- ✓ Are you making eye contact with the interviewer at all times?
- ✓ Have you used hand gestures where appropriate?
- ✓ Did you express your ideas in a logical sequence, following the PEP approach?
- ✓ Did you express your opinions clearly?
- ✓ Have you described the skills you gained through the Link Modules activities?
- ✓ Have you used action words when describing events, e.g. I planned, we evaluated?
- ✓ Is your uniform neat and are you dressed appropriately?
- ✓ Is the interview area appropriate?

If you are happy with your recording, submit it as part of your portfolio. Photocopy the sequence sheet and submit it with your portfolio, highlighting your Leaving Certificate number. Remember, submit your **best** work for assessment.

The Written Examination

It can be difficult to achieve a distinction in the LCVP, so it is extremely important to revise and prepare adequately for the written examination. You must practise questions and be aware of the marking schemes, which are available on the website of the State Examinations Commission.

The written examination, which is worth 160 marks, is held on the first Wednesday in May of the second year of the Leaving Certificate programme. The portfolio of coursework, which is prepared mainly during class time over the two years of the programme, is worth 240 marks. This must be presented on the first Wednesday in March.

> Section A and Section B are compulsory, which means you must answer the audio-visual and case study questions.

When answering questions in the written paper, you must follow a logical sequence. Use the learning cycle approach (PEP: pre-experience, experience and post-experience) and articulate the knowledge and skills gained. You need to be familiar with all of the 93 specific learning outcomes (SLOs).

The written examination lasts for two and a half hours and is comprised of three sections.

Section A: Audio-Visual Presentation (30 Marks)

This usually profiles a business, a local area or business enterprise or a voluntary organisation. The six-minute presentation on DVD is shown at the beginning of the examination. You must then answer eight questions. You are assessed on:

- **What you see:** For example, the staff in the organisation may be working in teams.
- **What you hear:** The entrepreneur mentioned the qualities she would like when employing staff.
- **Applying your LCVP knowledge, skills and learning:** The entrepreneur may mention one issue on the DVD, but the question may ask you to discuss the issues that this business faces. As an LCVP student, you should be aware of many issues that a business could encounter.

Read the **eight** questions carefully before the DVD starts and underline the **main parts**. Take notes on the rough work sheet on the inside cover of the answer booklet. Remember, the last few questions carry a substantial amount of the marks. In fact, Question 7 and Question 8 are worth 12 marks. Therefore, they require a lot of detail, so be sure to elaborate and always give examples if appropriate. Try structuring your answer before you start. Use a mind map.

Section B: Case Study (30 Marks)

The case study is a descriptive account of a person, an enterprise (business, community or voluntary organisation), your local area or a socioeconomic issue.

The case study arrives in your school approximately four weeks before the written exam. When you receive your copy, make good use of the opportunity to understand and analyse the case study. You need to have a good understanding of the case study, as you will only have approximately 25 minutes to answer questions on it. You are required to answer three questions. The three questions may also have multiple parts to them, with two to three subdivisions in each question.

Read the questions carefully. **Stop and think**. **Underline** the important parts. Give details and always **elaborate**.

You can also use the case study as a revision tool for the other questions in the written paper by applying the specific learning outcomes (SLOs). Quite a few of the SLOs can be applied naturally to any case study. This can be achieved by revisiting the SLOs and using the case study to apply the learning outcomes, e.g. identify support available to this organisation, how could I secure a work placement?, how could we organise a visit out to this organisation?, how can they ensure targets are reached? Receiving the case study in advance helps to prevent blanks on the day of the exam.

Resources

Past exam papers and exam videos

Business 2000

Exploring Enterprise

Newspapers (national and local)

You can decide to write your own case study, e.g. on a visit in or visit out, voluntary organisation, community enterprise, business enterprise, 'My Own Place', enterprise activities, etc.
In the LCVP you are assessed on two cases:

- Audio-visual – Section A of the written paper
- Written case – Section B of the written paper

Both of these cases are **compulsory**. Using case studies is an important part of the LCVP.

How to prepare for the case study

You will receive the case study in advance of the written exam, but you will only receive the questions on the day of the exam. The following is an ideal way to prepare for the case study questions.

1. **Read** the case study.
   - Skim read to gain an understanding and a general sense of the case study.
   - Read it a second time and underline the difficult words, business words and LCVP-related words. Make sure you can explain these words with examples if appropriate. Make sure you are able to write at least three different points about the use or significance of these words, as there may be full questions on them.
2. Prepare a **SWOT/SCOT** analysis.
   - SWOT: Strengths, weaknesses, opportunities and threats (see page 144)
   - SCOT: Strengths, challenges, opportunities and threats
3. Identify problems and make decisions. Use **brainstorming** to list all possible problems.

Tip: How many SLOs can you apply to the case study?

- What would you do to solve these problems?
- List the different courses of action.
- Prioritise problems – which problem is the most significant and why?

4. Prepare a profile on the following: **people**, **organisation** and **place**.
   - People: Prepare a profile on qualities, skills and experiences.
   - Organisation: Is it a business, community enterprise or voluntary organisation? Is it a sole trader, partnership or company?
   - Place: Does location matter?

5. Prepare a **summary and/or presentation**. For example, try to reduce the first five lines to one line.

How many SLOs can you apply to the case study?

To become familiar with the case studies that have been used in previous years, use exam papers and suggested solutions. You can try to anticipate possible questions, but it is more important to have an **in-depth understanding of the case study**.

By using the above methodology and using the case study to revise **all** the specific learning outcomes, you will have a deeper understanding of it. Then, regardless of what questions come up, you will be able to answer them and suggest appropriate solutions.

Remember that in the assessment you will have to write down the solutions to questions. This is a different skill to oral discussion and it is important to practise it. Use your LCVP folder to write down solutions and you will be better prepared when it comes to the exam.

Overview of how to prepare for the case study

1. Read the case study	Skim read Underline words	Develop a sense of the case. Get a feel for it. ■ Difficult words ■ Business words ■ LCVP-related words
2. Prepare a SWOT/SCOT analysis	Strengths Weaknesses/Challenges Opportunities Threats	Internal, e.g. staff Internal, e.g. machinery External, e.g. new markets External, e.g. competition
3. Identify problems and make decisions	List the problems Prioritise the problems	Give solutions: what would you do? Identify the biggest problem
4. Prepare a POP profile	People Organisation Place	
5. Prepare a summary	Reduce the first five sentences to one, etc.	

Case study preparation should be an integral part of the LCUP over the two years.

Section C: General Questions (4 X 25 Marks)

There are six multi-part general questions covering the full range of the syllabus. You are required to answer four of the questions. To help you choose the questions, the examination paper has a summary and index of questions. Your choice of questions is vital. Choose the questions that can deliver the most marks for you. Make sure you can answer **all** the parts. Take account of mark allocations for questions and parts of questions and plan your use of time accordingly.

Pay particular attention to timing. Don't spend too much time on one part of the question. You should allow approximately **23 minutes per question**.

If you find yourself going over the time, leave it and move on to the next question. If there's time at the end of the examination, you can always return to it.

Always **define** your answer, **explain** your answer, give at least two different points and **give an example** supporting your answer. Don't leave blank spaces – attempt all parts of the four questions.

> Use the DEE approach: define, explain and give an example if appropriate.

> **Tip:** Have you completed the twenty sample questions at the end of each unit?

Revising Exam Questions: Some Important Themes

When revising or practising exam questions, use Venn diagrams to practise compare and contrast-type questions, to explain the similarities and differences between things or to distinguish between two concepts. This is an excellent tool to help you structure your answer.

> **Tip:** Draft the diagram to structure your answer, then start writing your answer.

Venn Diagram

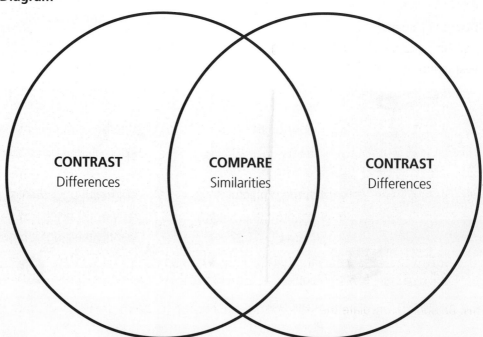

CONTRAST
Differences

COMPARE
Similarities

CONTRAST
Differences

Compare similarities – what is common to both
Contrast differences – distinguish what is unique to each

Make sure you understand the differences between common terms
that frequently appear on the written paper, such as state, explain, outline,
analyse, describe, discuss, evaluate and illustrate.

See the
examination
terms on
page 208.

- **State** simply means to say briefly or define what a term means.
- If **explaining**, ask yourself, 'Would another person understand this concept/idea/term now that I have explained it? Have I made it clear?'
- To **outline** means to give a complete overview, so you need to cover the entire concept. This is why a brief outline is often asked for.
- **Analysing** means breaking something down into its constituent parts.
- To **describe** something is like drawing a picture with words.
- A **discussion** looks at something from a number of sides or from a number of points of view.
- To **evaluate** something means to make a judgement on it. Make sure your judgement is informed, i.e. you must be able to back it up with evidence. List advantages, benefits, disadvantages and risks.
- To **illustrate** means to show and give examples.

Tip: When answering questions, discuss information from your portfolio where appropriate.

A few important themes that are an integral part of the LCVP.

- **Planning** is an integral part of the LCVP. Make sure to cover all areas of planning:
  - Define planning.
  - Why plan?
  - List the advantages and challenges associated with a plan.
  - Can you draft a business plan? What are the main headings?
  - Can you draft an enterprise/action plan?

Tip: These are covered in Section 1.

- **Evaluation** is also an integral part of the LCVP. Make sure to answer questions carefully.
  - Why evaluate?
  - Discuss the advantages and challenges of evaluating an activity and a portfolio item, etc.
  - How to evaluate?
  - List the advantages and disadvantages of different methods of evaluating.

Only use
mnemonics if
they suit your
learning style.

When evaluating, use the **DAR** approach.

- **Describe:** Reflect on the experience. What happened? What did you do? Did you meet your objectives?
- **Assess:** Think back on the experience. What went well? What did not work? Was it useful? What subjects were useful? What about teamwork?
- **Recommend:** What would you recommend for future activities? Are there any follow-on activities?

- **Skills:** Be able to articulate the skills you developed. The following are skills you developed as

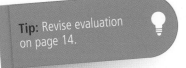

Tip: Revise evaluation on page 14.

you participated in the LCVP:
- Communication skills
- Teamwork skills
- Organisation skills
- Research skills
- Administrative skills
- Presentation skills
- Information technology skills

- Revise enterprising skills and be able to compare and contrast skills and qualities.

Tip: Revise pages 12–14.

Remember, the LCVP has two Link Modules: Preparation for the World of Work and Enterprise Education.

Legislation

There are three specific pieces of legislation on the syllabus:
- Safety, Health and Welfare at Work Act
- Employment Equality Act
- Protection of Young Persons (Employment) Act

Tip: Revise legislation on pages 32–34.

There are other pieces of legislation that you may decide to describe in your answers.

Activities

The LCVP is an **activity-based programme**. Be aware of all the activities:

- Visit in or visit out
- 'My Own Place' investigation
- Simulated job interviews
- Career investigations and local business investigations
- Work placements
- Presentations/interviews
- Voluntary/community organisation investigations
- Enterprise activity

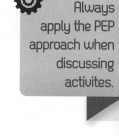

Always apply the PEP approach when discussing activites.

Important Tips

Read questions carefully. **Common mistakes** can lead to misinterpreting the question. The following are examples:

- Is the question on a visit in or a visit out?
- Are you being asked to evaluate the organising of an event or evaluate the organisation?
- Are you evaluating the career or the activity itself, i.e. the career investigation?
- Why evaluate an activity vs. evaluating an activity
- Work experience vs. work placement
- Know the differences between strengths, weaknesses, opportunities and threats. Make sure you can draft a SWOT analysis for an entrepreneur, business or voluntary organisation that you studied.
- What makes an activity successful vs. discussing the activity

- The role of the entrepreneur vs. the role of the manager
- How to improve on a skill, rather than describing the skill
- Entrepreneur skills, qualities and characteristics
- Personal risks vs. business risks when establishing a business
- Business plan and enterprise/action plan
- Obligations of an employer and employee
- What makes a business successful vs. measuring the success of a business

And finally:

- Be aware of all 93 specific learning outcomes (SLOs).
- Revise your portfolio, as this is an excellent revision tool. Refer to the learning, skills and knowledge gained.
- Read all questions carefully and answer all the required parts.
- Always define, explain at least two different points and give an example.
- Take a critical look at each answer before moving on to ensure that all the relevant details are included.
- Use the learning gained through the completion of the portfolio.
- Take account of mark allocations for questions and parts of questions and plan your use of time accordingly.
- Use the published marking scheme as a resource and a guide when preparing for the written examination.

How to Answer Questions

Question: Outline the issues that arise for this voluntary organisation.

Read the question carefully. Underline the outcome verb or the word that indicates the type of answer required.

Outline the issues that arise for this voluntary organisation.

'Outline' is an outcome verb that requires you to write a short summary of the important features.

Next, underline the key words needed for the answer.

Outline the <u>issues</u> that arise for this *voluntary organisation*.

For example, you could discuss issues such as finance, resources and lack of volunteers and write a paragraph on each point.

Finally, look back over your answer to make sure all the necessary key words are included.

It is very important to give at least three points. Elaborate and have specific examples.

Revise layouts:

- Portfolio
- Business plan (page 140)
- Letter (page 55)
- Agenda/minutes (page 130)
- SWOT (page 144)
- Marketing mix (page 172)
- E-mail (page 53)
- Contract of employment (page 28)
- Questionnaire (page 171)

Tip: Revise the twenty sample questions on pages 20, 47, 70, 92, 114, 134, 152, 164 and 185.

Possible Marking Scheme for Core Portfolio Items (All 4 Must Be Submitted)

1. Curriculum vitae	Marks
Word-processing	0–2
Presentation/layout (conventional order)	0–3
Personal details (any four items, including signature)	0–4
Skills and qualities	0–2
Educational qualifications	0–3
Work experience	0–3
Achievements/interests/hobbies	0–5
Referees	0–3
Subtotal	**25**

2. Enterprise/action plan	Marks
Presentation and layout	0–3
Title/purpose	0–2
Objectives (at least two needed)	0–4
Research methods	0–2
Analysis of research	0–6
Action steps	0–6
Schedule of time/costs	0–6
Evaluation methods	0–6
Subtotal	**35**

3. Career investigation	Marks
Title/word-processing/use of headings (or audio tape communication in clear and confident manner)	0–5
Description of duties involved in the career/area	0–3
Identification of skills and qualities needed	0–5
Identification of qualifications and training needed	0–5
What was learned by the research/activity about the career and oneself?	0–8
Description of two different pathways to the career	0–4
Evaluation of the career	0–5
Evaluation of undertaking the career investigation	0–5
Subtotal	**40**

4. Summary report	Marks
Presentation layout	1–5
Title/name of activity	0–5
Author's name	0/5
Terms of reference of report/aims of the activity	0/3/5
Body of report – content (short sentences, summaries, appropriate language)	1–10
Body of report – clarity (headings, logical structure, flow, originality of thought)	1–5
Conclusions/recommendations	1–5
Subtotal	**40**

Note that the marking schemes may change. Follow the guidelines and marking schemes on the State Examinations Commission website.

MAXIMUM 140 MARKS

Possible Marking Scheme for Optional Portfolio Items (2 out of 4 Must Be Submitted)

1. Diary of work experience

	Marks
Presentation/layout	0–5
Name and description of work experience placement	0–5
Reasons for choosing work experience placement	0–5
Content	
Factual day-to-day account of at least three days/entries, as follows:	
■ Detailed personalised account	0–10
■ Candidate analysis of own performance in different situations	0–10
Expression and evaluation	
Evaluation of experience in the light of study and career aspirations	0–5
Evaluation of how what has been learned can be applied to work in the home, school and the local community	0–10
Subtotal	**50**

2. Enterprise report

	Marks
Presentation/layout	0–4
Title/table of contents	0–2
Author's name or signature	0–2
Terms of reference of report/aims of activity	0–4
Summary of main points	0–4
Body of report (may include personal contribution)	
Account of activity	0–10
Use of appropriate depth, detail, organisation of information	0–8
Use of charts, tables, diagrams	0–4
Conclusions/recommendations	0–6
Evaluations	0–6
Subtotal	**50**

3. 'My Own Place' report

	Marks
Presentation/layout	0–4
Title/table of contents	0–2
Description of local area/what is under investigation	0–5
Aim/objectives	0–5
Research methods	0–5
Body of report – description and analysis of key aspects	0–6
Use of logical sequence/headings/illustrations	0–5
Analysis of issue/suggestions for improvements	0–6
Conclusions and recommendations	0–6
Evaluation	0–6
Subtotal	**50**

4. Recorded interview/presentation

	Marks
Presentation (neat in the context of the interview/presentation)	0–4
Variety of tone, gesture, diction, eye contact	0–4
Ability to communicate message clearly, engage audience, elaborate on points/questions, logical sequence of thought	0–36
Pass (18–23) – basic communication skills	
Merit (24–27) – ability to express ideas and opinions clearly and knowledge of topic	
Distinction (28–36) – knowledge and ability to communicate ideas and own opinions clearly and in logical sequence	
Information (content)	0–6
Subtotal	**50**

ANY TWO OPTIONS (MAXIMUM 100 MARKS)

LCVP Assessment Words

The following terms appear frequently in the general questions. It is really important to understand the meaning of each term before you can attempt answers.

Term	Definition
Analyse	To study a problem in detail by breaking it down into its various parts and examining possible relationships
Apply	To bring knowledge or skills into use for a particular purpose
Characteristics	Distinguishing qualities or attributes of an individual or object
Comment on	To express an opinion about something
Compare	To examine two or more things in order to discover their similarities
Contrast	To show the difference(s) between something
Criterion	A standard by which something can be judged or decided
Define	To state the precise meaning of
Describe	To give an account of a person, relationship, event, organisation or location
Draft	To draw up a document, letter or report
Evaluate	To find or determine the worth, value or significance of something; to assess or make a judgement
Explain	To make clear in a detailed way
Identify	To show recognition of something
Illustrate	To make clear by using examples, charts, diagrams, etc.
Indicate	To point out or state briefly
List	To write down a number of names or objects that have something in common
Mention	To refer to briefly
Outline	To give a short summary of the important features of a subject
Qualities	The distinguishing characteristics or attributes of an individual or object
Suggest	To put forward an idea or plan